CW00923284

Irvin D. Yalom

On Psychotherapy
and the Human Condition

Ruthellen Josselson, Ph.D.

Jorge Pinto Books Inc.
New York

*Irvin D. Yalom: On Psychotherapy and the Human Condition*

Published by Jorge Pinto Books Inc.,
  website: www.pintobooks.com

Cover design © 2007 by Nigel Holmes,
  website: www.nigelholmes.com

Irvin Yalom back cover photograph by Joseph Siroker.

Book design by Charles King,
  website: www.ckmm.com

ISBN 978-0-9795576-1-3
  0-9795576-1-5

Working Biographies

# Acknowledgments

I am deeply grateful to Irv Yalom for his availability and candor as well as his help in producing this work. I wish to thank several of my students at the Fielding Graduate University for reading, commenting on and editing an earlier draft of the manuscript: Katanya Good, Gillian Karp, Marguerite Laban, and Suzanne McKann. And I thank Marilyn Yalom for her careful editing of the final version.

# Contents

# Introduction

Irvin Yalom is one of the best known, most widely read and most influential psychiatrists in the contemporary world. Through his many books, which are accessible to ordinary readers as well as illuminating for psychotherapists, he has provided a guide for living in a perplexing world. A recent poll of American psychotherapists voted him to be one of the three most important living therapists, but the worldwide success of his books suggests that his prominence is international.

Rather than positioning himself as a representative of one of the hundreds of "schools" or approaches to psychotherapy, Yalom offers a message that goes to the heart of psychotherapy. Taking up the central existential concerns of human life, Yalom's work engages the problems of finding meaning in life and confronting death, concerns that had lain beyond the scope of psychiatry.

Writing in a literary style that reviewers have compared to Freud, Yalom details what actually happens in the intimate human encounter that is psychotherapy. Yalom does not shrink from exposing his own thoughts and feelings about what occurs; he, too, is a vulnerable and searching human being. He makes his thinking about his patients, and his efforts to treat them, transparent, exposing his doubts, reservations and struggles as well as his insights. He has written two textbooks, two volumes of case history stories, three novels about therapy, a guide for therapists and one book of counsel for the masses confronting death. Across all of this work, he explores the limitless and complex possibilities of the healing inherent in genuine human connection and authentic awareness of the dilemmas of human existence. His writing is intellectually enlightening as well as deeply moving. While he has received many awards, he would most value the millions of individual lives that he has touched.

***

I first encountered Irvin Yalom through his writing when I was a clinical psychology intern in 1970. The Massachusetts Mental Health Center, where I was in training, was an august bastion of psychoanalytic thought, but I walked through the halls clutching Yalom's *The Theory and Practice of Group Psychotherapy* as ammunition with which to challenge the prevailing orthodoxy of this institution. In those days, Yalom espoused a radical approach to psychotherapy that advocated the importance of the human relationship between therapist and patient and located the action of psychotherapy in interpersonal learning. These were incendiary ideas in those times where people were still debating the implications of therapists saying "Good morning" to patients for fear this would disrupt the transference of infantile experiences from patients onto therapists. The idea that therapists could create a very human and humane relationship with patients and be even more effective rather than less, that the focus of therapy could be in the nature of adult relationships that patients were creating with the people in their lives, that therapists could talk genuinely with patients about the shared dilemmas of the human condition—these were subversive ideas. The book was, of course, greeted with contempt by my professors and supervisors but it heralded a sea change in my generation who saw the wisdom it contained, and we modified our understanding of our work, slowly and over the years, accordingly. Today, when I read contemporary relational psychoanalysis, I see that psychoanalysis is only now, thirty years later, discovering what Yalom was teaching back then.

Indeed, *The Theory and Practice of Group Psychotherapy*, now in its 5th edition, is probably the most widely read work in all of mental health practice. It has been translated into seventeen languages.

But Yalom's influence has not been limited to psychotherapy practitioners. He has distilled his insight about the problems of existence into several novels that have had worldwide appeal to people outside the psychotherapy professions. Daily, he receives letters and emails from people in many countries detailing the ways in which reading his work has changed their lives.

Ten years after my first encounter with Yalom's writing, in a period of despair in my own life, I read *Existential Psychotherapy*, his next most classic work. The wisdom in this book seemed to speak directly to me as I was grappling with questions about meaning and isolation. Reading what he had to say, it was as if he were in the room with me, offering me courage and hope. I experienced him, through reading, as a consoling friend, someone who had been to the same dark places and found some light. So I became one of the thousands who have written to him over the years, thanking him for writing what he did and telling him how much he had helped me. And, to my astonishment, he wrote back. (This was before email so there was the necessity of addressing envelopes and finding a stamp.) Thus began a friendship and colleagueship that has endured for 27 years.

Recognizing his uniqueness and specialness within the field of psychiatry and beyond, I set out, in this biographical project, to understand the roots of his particular form of wisdom—and his capacity to communicate it to others. What path has led him to such a nuanced and insightful understanding of the problems of being human?

In writing this intellectual biography, I am aware, as are perhaps all biographers of extraordinary human beings, of the problems of accounting for genius. Genius is itself an emergent phenomenon that is not a simple summation of the parts that compose it. Creativity involves shepherding something new into existence, something that takes available materials of the world and shapes them into a form that leads us to see the world differently. Yalom's virtuosity has resided in a particular capacity to meld philosophy, literature and psychiatry into a corpus of work that illuminates life-as-lived for all human beings and, especially, for those who treat their mental distress. In this intellectual biography, I try to trace the roots, the fertilization and the fruits of his thought.

Part of Yalom's appeal is the way he articulates in simple language the deepest aspects of human reality. I have chosen, therefore, to preserve his voice wherever possible, and have structured this biography as a mixture of interview material, quotations from his writings, and my own synopses of his ideas.

# 1

# Origins[1]

*"If we meditate on our being alive, our existing in the world and we try to just put aside all other distractions, all lesser matters, and we try to get down to the bedrock from which anxiety springs, we get to certain concerns—death, meaninglessness, isolation and freedom. I think in those terms all the time. I take them very seriously. I've never gone too far from the basic skeleton of the* Existential Psychotherapy *book, which focuses on these concerns."* —Irvin D. Yalom

    I begin to trace Irvin Yalom's intellectual development by reproducing a slightly edited interview I conducted with him about the origins of his approach to psychiatry and psychotherapy. I think it important for the reader to get to know him through his own words about himself. The printed transcript, of course, omits the music of his rich, expressive voice, which the reader will have to imagine.

    For Yalom, it was Rollo May's book *Existence* that

opened up a new vista. He was then a resident in psychiatry and reading this book led him to take courses in
philosophy at Johns Hopkins University. It was difficult
for a psychiatry resident to be spending three evenings
a week with a survey of Western philosophy, but he
read every word of Bertrand Russell's *History of Western
Philosophy*.

This was a new world for Yalom who, growing up
in a working class family, had never studied philosophy
before. As a child, he lived in a Washington, D.C. slum,
above his father's store where it was dangerous to walk
down the block. When he was 14, the family moved to a
comfortable and safe neighborhood in Washington and
he attended a better school. But he had few guides along
the way as he created a new approach to psychotherapy
based in a deep appreciation for the dilemmas of the
human condition.

*Irv Yalom:*   For reasons that now seem incomprehensible
to me, during college I was in a terrible hurry
and very anxious about getting into medical
school. These were the days of a quota for
Jewish students, a 5% quota in medical school
classes. George Washington University had
a class of 100 and they could only accept
five Jews. And so I was very anxious, probably more so than ever in my life, about my
future. So pressed was I that I applied to be
admitted after only three years of college. You
could do that at some medical schools. My

guiding principle at that point was to get all A's so they'd have to take me, and that's what happened.

*Ruthellen:* How come getting into medical school then was so important, so central?

*Irv Yalom:* I don't think I really saw any other choices in life. I lived in a cultural ghetto. There was no realistic view of the outside world, really. I had no advisors, no counselors. I felt, as did all my peers, that was the only way out of the ghetto.

*Ruthellen:* Medical school?

*Irv Yalom:* Medical school. The only way I could see. Otherwise you went into business with your father, and the third choice is that you would do something less demanding than medical school, perhaps dental school. I had no vision that one could do anything else and I don't think I was alone in this.

*Ruthellen:* So it was about moving up economically rather than helping people or doing—

*Irv Yalom:* No, no, it wasn't moving up economically. That wasn't at all the issue. The issue was getting out of the ghetto, just entering the modern world, expanding my vision, entering another kind of life. My father and mother were hard working, amazingly hard working, and by the time I was in college were making a relatively comfortable living from their liquor and grocery store. It wasn't the money. I knew even then I'd have been wealthier by going into business. It was the intellectual life, the literary life that beckoned me. I was a voracious reader from as early as I can remember, and I wanted to find some kind of entry into that world. If I wanted to get in to Tolstoy's world, I must have thought, then the only way I could do it was through the portals of medical school. And once getting into medical school, then I would go into psychiatry and that would get me closer and closer to the life of the mind. That was always the idea.

*Ruthellen:*   From the vantage point of who you were in the ghetto—what did you think psychiatry was? What was your view, as much as you can reconstruct it?

*Irv Yalom:*   I don't remember reading anything at that point, but I remember thinking that psychiatry was the study of the mind, the study of the way that we think, and in undergraduate school, I must have—I can't remember—I must have taken a course in abnormal psychology. My memory is hazy and I'm not sure about that because I was taking a straight pre-med curriculum.

*Ruthellen:* So this was the late '40s, right, that you were in college?

*Irv Yalom:* Yeah. In 1949 to 1952. In my three years of college, because the pre-medical requirements were so heavy, I think I had a total of four electives, and every single one of them was in literature. I took things that fit into my tight schedule such as American poetry and world drama. So I was stretching toward literature but I had no idea how one could fashion a life in literature.

*Ruthellen:* Did you know anybody who was a psychiatrist? There weren't TV programs in the—

*Irv Yalom:* No I didn't.

*Ruthellen:* I was just thinking about how you could even have gotten access to a concept of what psychiatry was then? Because in the early '50s, it looked very different than it looks now. Psychoanalysis was really just starting to take hold in the postwar era.

*Irv Yalom:* I didn't know anything about that in college. I wish I had—some therapy for my anxiety would have been a blessing then. I'm more clear about how I decided to become a doctor. First there is this desire that you already have suggested of wanting to be helpful and useful to people.

My father had a heart attack when I was about 14. I know the date quite precisely. I remember 'cause I wanted to go to summer camp that summer, which I couldn't because of having to stay home with him while my mother worked in the store. But I took a summer school course in trigonometry, which at that point, was a junior high school course.

I remember the night of his coronary with great clarity. It was the middle of the night and my mother and I were home. And she was out of control, very distraught and, as she was so often prone to do, looking for someone to take the blame and that was me. So she was yelling at me, "You killed him. You're responsible. It's your behavior and your making trouble that caused this."

And I was anxiously cowering in the corner waiting for the doctor, Benjamin Manchester, to arrive. I had such relief when I heard the sound of his tires scraping the curb in front of my home. I remember his round friendly face as clear as if it were yesterday. He was wonderfully reassuring; he tousled my hair, and let me listen to my father's heart through the stethoscope, assuring me that his heartbeat was as regular as a clock and he was going to be fine.

This may be all reconstruction, but I felt like then and there I made the decision that I was going to go to medical school and try to offer others what Dr. Manchester had offered. So there were two streams that shaped my ambitions—being a doctor and being a writer.

*Ruthellen:* Tell me more about the part of you that thought maybe you'd become a writer.

*Irv Yalom:* I scribbled a lot of poetry during these years and always liked to write. And I did well in any kind of a course—this goes back to elementary school—in which there was some kind of writing exercise. It was always my paper that was held up, or read aloud by the teacher or was pinned on the bulletin board. That was the one way I excelled in school.

And I could always tell a good story, so whenever we had some sort of show and tell, the story that I would tell generally captivated the audience. I had a large repository of stories because I avidly read. One of my hobbies in childhood was collecting old copies of *Reader's Digest.*

I had an enormous collection of *Reader's Digests* and I would bike down to the 7th and K Central Library in Washington to fill my saddle bags with my library books for the week. But then about a block away, there were a couple of used book stores which, among other things, sold old *Reader's Digests.* And sometimes they were expensive, like $3.00 or $4.00 each and I never could afford the oldest ones. As I recall, the magazine started in 1921 and I had a fairly complete collection from about '27 on.

The *Reader's Digest* would have these strange little stories or odd curiosities, often a couple of paragraphs of people's stories of unusual or life-changing events that had happened to them. I used a lot of those stories in my stories that I would tell to the class.

In college, I did little writing because the university I went to, George Washington, had such large classes that teachers rarely assigned written papers.

*Ruthellen:* Well, back to high school and your telling stories—do you remember a particular time of telling a story that was special, memorable, or stands out for you during that time?

*Irv Yalom:* There was an English teacher that I had named Miss McCauley. Marilyn (my wife, who I met in high school) had her, too. And she adored Marilyn and I think she detested me for hanging around and distracting Marilyn all the time. She referred to me as a locker cowboy.

Marilyn was darling, the class valedictorian, a star in journalism, student government, and all other school activities. She had such social grace that she had many teachers who took a special interest in her. But I was a very jittery nerd at that time and always felt unattractive and embarrassed about my appearance. Today when I look back on pictures of myself, I see myself as a fairly attractive young man and am struck by my distortions of my appearance. Miss McCauley was extraordinarily critical of me. Very recently, when looking through souvenirs I discovered a paper I wrote in her tenth or eleventh grade English class. It was a poetic lyrical homage to baseball. I was a big baseball fan then.

Her criticism was scathing. She despised the fact that I had so much emotion for such a trivial thing and gave me a B minus on the top and peppered my paper with red marks ridiculing my enthusiasm. She was absolutely stifling, such a horrible example of a teacher who should be inspiring a student. It almost brought me to tears, even now, reading her criticism. A story I've considered writing but never have, concerns a boy who had a teacher like Miss McCauley and conceived the plan of returning to her years later in triumph flaunting all his books and signs of success. He'd show her alright. When he did finally return to his old high school he learned, of course, that she had been dead for years.

*Ruthellen:*  Were there other, enabling teachers?

*Irv Yalom:*  I never really felt I had an enabling teacher during my childhood and adolescence. I wish I had. In the last few years I've been aware of a fantasy that comes to me sometimes when I'm biking or walking that feels very powerful. Once it starts I can't stop it: it takes on a life of its own. The fantasy is this:

I'm in junior high school and some teacher comes into my parents' store, tells them that I'm a very exceptional student and they should transfer me to a decent school, to some privileged private school. My parents agree—they always encouraged my education—and this teacher becomes my mentor: he takes a special interest in my writing and encourages me to join the school baseball and tennis team.

*Ruthellen:* And nobody took that special interest?

*Irv Yalom:* No, nobody did. No teacher I ever had, certainly through high school and college. No teacher whatsoever.

*Ruthellen:* So what kept you going?

*Irv Yalom:* Well, there's a very, very important role played in my life by Marilyn. We're talking now about tenth grade, which is about when I met her: she was a year behind me and I attended her valedictorian address in junior high school. We started going steady when I was about fifteen. She was a kindred spirit and when we were together, we'd often talk about literature. We'd talk about Dostoevsky and Steinbeck and Thomas Wolfe. She was the only person I knew who read like I did. She was exceedingly important in my formative years. But she had something that I didn't have, which is that she had several mentors.

She had high school teachers who took her under their wing. One was the journalism teacher who mentored her and appointed her editor-in-chief of the school newspaper. She had another teacher, her French teacher, who made it quite clear to her that she was to go to Wellesley, whereas when I graduated high school I had no idea about any other college in the country except my local ones.

My brother-in-law, my sister's husband, went to George Washington University and then GW medical school. He was a fine doctor and if GW was good enough for him it was, I felt, good enough for me and I applied nowhere else. I was a reasonably good student in high school, probably in the top five of the class and got a scholarship to GW, which covered the three hundred dollar annual tuition. So, no, I never had any kind of a mentor.

In college also I was an anonymous student. I had no personal contact with any of my teachers. In college, I made only one B (in German). I not only made A's, but disrupted the class curve. Whereas the 2nd highest grade might be an 85 or a 90, I was at 99. I was way, way off the class curve only because I was a fanatic student and studied like a demon. As I said, I was obsessed with getting all A's and so no one could stop me from getting into medical school.

I applied to twenty medical schools, after three years of college, with a near 4.0 grade average—and got turned down by 19. But I did get accepted at GW.

In medical school, too, I had no personal contact with any particular teacher. I don't recall having (or initiating) a conversation with a teacher. I compensated for this not only with my enabling relationship with Marilyn but with a very close relationship with a group of young men, two of whom continue to be my closest friends.

My first year of medical school was, without question, the worst year of my life. Marilyn was spending her junior year in France; I missed her a great deal and was overwhelmed with work and anxiety. I transferred at that point to Boston University to be near her.

But then, in medical school, when I took psychiatry, I experienced a turning point. We students were each assigned a patient for therapy and, one by one, each of us had to present our patient to a very august audience of about 20–25 faculty members, most of them from the Boston Psychoanalytic Institute.

*Ruthellen:*   This was your first case presentation.

*Irv Yalom:*   Right. I was pretty anxious about it. I remember my patient very clearly—a red headed, freckled woman, a few years older than I. I was to meet with her for eight weekly sessions (the length of the clerkship). In the first session she told me she was a lesbian.

That was not a good start because I didn't know what a lesbian was. I had never heard the term before. I made an instant decision that the only way I could really relate to her was to be honest and to tell her I didn't know what a lesbian was. So I asked her to enlighten me and over the eight weeks we developed a close relationship. She was the patient I presented to the faculty.

Now I had been to several of these conferences with other students and they were gut-wrenching. Each of these analysts would try to outdo the other with pompous complex formulations. They showed little empathy for the student who was often crushed by the merciless criticism.

I simply got up and talked about my patient and told it as a story. I don't think I even used any notes. I said here's how we met. Here's what she looked like. Here's what I felt. Here's what evolved. I told her of my ignorance. She educated me. I was profoundly interested in what she told me. She grew to trust me. I tried to help as best I could though I had few arrows of comfort in my quiver.

At the end of my talk there was a loud long total silence. I was puzzled. I had done something that was extremely easy and natural for me. And, one by one, the analysts—those guys who couldn't stop one-upping each other—said things to the effect of, "Well, this presentation speaks for itself. There's nothing we can say. It's a remarkable case. A startling and tender relationship." And all I had done was simply tell a story, which felt so natural and effortless for me. That was definitely an eye-opening experience: Then and there I knew I had found my place in the world.

This memory is perhaps a life-defining moment for Yalom. As he remembers and talks about it, he is deeply moved. In some ways, his work ever since has been about telling stories, stories about his encounters with people as a therapist, stories that instruct us about how to connect meaningfully with others. He has retained his essential humility—he still allows others to teach him about their reality as he tries to encounter them in their deepest being and offer them a relationship in which they can heal.

This moment also marked for Yalom a route out of the anonymity he had experienced throughout his education. Despite his academic successes, no one had recognized that he had any particular talent and he had only the vaguest sense that he had some special ability. For the first time, he was recognized—and for doing something that his teachers had never seen done before.

*Ruthellen:*   Where did you get the courage to do that?

*Irv Yalom:*   It didn't feel like anything courageous, as I recall—but this is over fifty years ago—I didn't have other options. It was my turn to present a case, this was my way to present a case. Whenever afterward I presented a case, whenever I presented at grand rounds or a lecture, I had the audience's full attention. I always had that ability.

*Ruthellen:*   So this moment when you told the case to the analysts and they were silent, they were unable to respond in their usual ways and start to compete with each other with formulations, you felt that they saw in you and that you had done something worth noticing, something important?

*Irv Yalom:* Oh, yeah, for sure. If I try to understand it now across all those decades, I think it was because I was talking about a psychiatric case, but speaking in a whole different realm, a literary, story-telling realm. And their formulations had no sway. The jargon, the interpretations, all that had nothing to do with the story I told them. Of course that's my view: I'd love to go back in time and learn what they were really thinking.

*Ruthellen:* There are so many different ways to tell a story, including the usual case presentation, which is also a way to tell a story. But this was a different way to tell a story.

*Irv Yalom:* I didn't know anything about telling a story or what telling a story meant in any kind of technical way, but I somehow knew how to put things together to create a drama.

*Ruthellen:* With yourself in it.

*Irv Yalom:* Oh, with myself in it. How I met her, how I didn't know anything about her being a lesbian, how baffled I was, how I guessed she must feel to work with a therapist who's admitted that he's totally ignorant of her lifestyle, how she must have worried about my accepting her, how I must have given to her some representative of the whole world who knew nothing about her and who possibly might ostracize her in some way.

Ruthellen: You didn't judge her, or pathologize her, or do something like that. You were able, in fact, to engage with her in a very human way.

Irv Yalom: Yes. I think that's true. I did not ostracize her—just the opposite, my confessing my ignorance drew us closer together—a relationship forged in honesty.

Ruthellen: As opposed to the psychiatric way or psychoanalytic way that would look at her as a carrier of symptoms and pathology.

Irv Yalom: That's right, case formulations that focus narrowly on pathology were very distasteful to me.

Ruthellen: It was distasteful even in medical school?

Irv Yalom: Even in medical school—I didn't like the distant disinterested stance of many psychiatrists I encountered.

Ruthellen: But you were still clear you wanted to go into psychiatry even though what they were doing was not something that you felt was at all appealing.

*Irv Yalom:* That's right. Once or twice I wavered because there were so many things I liked about medicine. I liked taking care of people, liked passing on to them what Dr. Manchester had passed on to me. But I never seriously entertained doing anything else in medicine. So I was committed. At this point, I was already starting to read a lot about psychiatry.

*Ruthellen:* What were you reading?

*Irv Yalom:* Well, textbooks of psychiatry. I was fascinated by any text that presented things in a slightly more humanistic fashion. I think maybe Robert Lindner's book came out then—*The Fifty-Minute Hour.*

And there was a textbook of principles and practice by Jules Masserman that was most enlightening because it took a different path. I haven't looked at this book ever since then, but I remember he talked about "ur-beliefs," the more fundamental existential assumptions about life.

*Ruthellen:* Well, what you've been describing is a strong literary sensibility that led you to medical school. You had been forming a sense of how people are through very deep identification with novels.

*Irv Yalom:* Yes, let me emphasize that throughout my life, from first reading *Treasure Island* when I had the mumps at the age of ten, I had constantly been reading novels. Since adolescence I have never *not* been reading a novel or story. Soon as I finish one, I go to another. I'd go to the library in Washington every week with bags of books I had digested and bring others home. My reading was omnivorous. It was entering another world, living in an alternate world. Probably because my childhood was so squalid, books had a desirable escapist quality for me.

*Ruthellen:* Squalid in what sense?

*Irv Yalom:* I lived in an awful place, it was rat infested. It was in a terrible neighborhood. The cockroaches were horrendous at our house. I was terrified of getting up in the middle of the night and turning on the light and seeing the big cockroaches scurrying around. Yeah, it was squalid. I've never overcome my phobia of cockroaches.

*Ruthellen:* So the escape was from the physical conditions, the bad physical conditions?

*Irv Yalom:* Well, and also from the psychological ones, too. In Washington, we were living in the middle of a black neighborhood. The only other white family was three of four blocks away at the next other grocery store. There I had someone with whom I would play, but he was a disagreeable boy. I had a dearth of friends. Mostly they were black children and my parents would not permit me to bring them into the house.

*Ruthellen:* Your school though was mainly white?

*Irv Yalom:* Oh yes, of course. Washington was entirely segregated in those days. Schools, even movies, restaurants, swimming pools, water fountains. Almost unbelievable to think of that now. My school was several blocks away. I'd cross over into the white district. My father's store was only about three blocks away from the dividing line, then it was white.

*Ruthellen:* Right, but oftentimes Jews were considered black for segregation purposes.

*Irv Yalom:* Well, I certainly was closer to some of the black boys in my neighborhood than to the redneck white boys, and often I was protected by the blacks from some of the rednecks, so I did have that experience, too. Yes there was definitely a much warmer bond between the Jews and blacks than there was between the

Jews and the non-Jewish white boys in the neighborhood.

*Ruthellen:* What about your sense of the larger would? This was wartime, after all. How did that have an impact on you?

*Irv Yalom:* Well, I remember following what I'd see in the news and the newsreel. I went to the movies very frequently. There was a little movie house, the Sylvan, a block from my father's store. In fact you didn't even cross a street. It was just around the corner. I'd go there three times a week. My parents were happy with anything that kept me off the streets. Usually there were double features and a lot of them were about the war, of course. And there were always newsreels about the war so that was mainly how I kept up with what was going on in the outside world.

My parents were *extremely* provincial. They were totally, totally submerged in the quest for survival and running this business, making enough money, trying to get out of the neighborhood, supporting their parents, and desperately concerned for the friends and relatives in the old country. There was, of course, no information available to them until after the war. And that was true for their

relatives and peers, too. They all lived above
or next to their store.

*Ruthellen:*  You were talking about books as a kind of escapist means for you. We got off on this thread
talking about what it is you may have been
wanting to escape, that there was something
about the alternate world and the way you
would feel being in the alternate worlds. But
it sounds like there was something else—you
wanted to learn how people are.

*Irv Yalom:*  Well, I can't deny that. In the D.C. Public
Library, on the first floor I was attracted by
a huge bookcase with hundreds and hundreds of books on biography. I started from
the A's on and read the weirdest range of
biographies.

In the A's I read a biography of Alexander the
Great, B's—Belmondo, the great bullfighter,
C—Ty Cobb and Constantine the Roman
emperor, G's—Hetty Green, who was called
the witch of Wall Street, a woman who was a
miser but had made millions on stock invest-
ments in Wall Street—and so on haphazardly
throughout the alphabet.

Yeah, so in retrospect, I must have been trying to find a way to learn about people and to

climb out of the ghetto. I had an amazingly ignorant, not unintelligent but uneducated group of relatives and peers. None of them were readers. I never knew any of them to ever read a book or talk about anything elevated, or go to a movie of some sort that was of any interest. I never saw either of my parents read a book. There wasn't a single person around me that I could look up to.

*Ruthellen:* So then back to this critical moment of presenting the case in medical school . . . I think it was a really important story because it was a moment that, besides your feeling of recognition, which was terribly important to you, it was also a first time of bringing your literary sensibility about people into contact with what was then the psychoanalytic establishment.

*Irv Yalom:* It was in medical school that I started reading Freud, a master story teller. You know he never won a Nobel prize (despite multiple nominations) but did win the Goethe prize for his literary abilities. Freud told great stories and I loved reading him until his acrobatic contortions at the ends of stories trying to fit his patients into his drive-based theory.

When I was a psychiatry resident at Johns

Hopkins, there were a couple of storytellers that used to consult with us whom I tremendously admired. They presented cases on a regular basis. The best of them all, the master story teller, was a psychiatrist named Otto Will. He would come and he'd just sit down without any notes and talk about some young patient that he had been seeing for five years. He used to hypnotize me and I hated for the hour to end. There was another psychiatrist almost as entrancing named Louis Hill. I admired them very much—I wanted to be like them when I grew up.

*Ruthellen:*  Because of their storytelling or because you thought that they helped you understand something?

*Irv Yalom:*  Oh, they were so *human.*

*Ruthellen:*  So human.

*Irv Yalom:*  They were human. They told their story in such human terms. There was not any jargon. There was no reduction of their patient in any way. They told a story of two people relating. I liked that very much. Harry Stack Sullivan said that psychotherapy was a relationship between two people—one of them more anxious than the other.

In my third year of residency I spent every Friday with John Whitehorn, the chairman of psychiatry at Hopkins. We watched him interview his patients in the hospital, spending an hour, or two, or three in which he asked patients about their life. They were not so much stories, but if they were coffee farmers, he'd want to know all about coffee, and how they grew it and what happened, and why was it better to plant coffee higher than lower. If the patient were a sixteenth century historian he'd spend hours inquiring about the origins and end of the Spanish Armada. Sometimes I grew impatient with his pace—he could not be rushed. But again and again I was startled to hear a patient slowly begin to reveal his psychotic thinking and the vast parameters of his paranoid system. John Whitehorn was a wise man. He was hostile to the current psychoanalytic ideas and jargon and built his own theories over and again. He used common sense, started out with each patient with a blank slate and figured out each person's story separately. He had no formula for people. I like that about him. In that way John Whitehorn lives on in me.

*Ruthellen:*   So let's talk about common sense and humanism. What you were bringing to this

reductionist, analytic field was humanism
and common sense with a literary sensibility,
a capacity to think about people living their
lives, and what it meant to them, and what
the encounter with *you* meant to them. And
that was true across what psychiatry—then as
now—would call the diagnostic spectrum. So
you would bring the same way of thinking to
people who seemed to be very disorganized
and to people who seemed to be quite high
functioning but nevertheless have some symptoms or distress. You weren't differentiating
even the neurotic and the psychotic?

*Irv Yalom:* No, no, I never liked to do that, which often
led to my having a lot of chutzpah about treating people who in the long run really weren't
reachable. We worked a lot with the severe
schizophrenic patients there, but I would try
every way I could to reach them.

*Ruthellen:* Did you feel you succeeded?

*Irv Yalom:* One patient suddenly comes to mind. I
haven't thought about her in over 30 years.
A woman named Sara. She was catatonic
and I'd meet with her every day of the week.
I had been taught that catatonic patients,
seemingly indifferent to their surroundings,
will nonetheless recall or record what's going

on. So I'd meet with her for about a half hour and chatter away, talking about my day and sharing my totally uninformed guesses about what she might be experiencing. She would never answer and stared blankly into space.

And then gradually after several months she emerged somewhat from the catatonia and I asked her about my visits and what they meant to her over the months. I said that I doubted they mattered because she never seemed to attend to me. I've never forgotten her response: "Oh, Dr. Yalom, you were my bread and butter during those days." That made a lasting impression on me: trust the relationship—you don't need to get an immediate response.

*Ruthellen:*  You were reaching people by trying to make yourself available.

*Irv Yalom:*  Yeah, I was concentrating on making myself available and learning from my experience. I'm afraid my iconoclasm resulted in my not taking advantage of most of my supervisors, especially those who took a passive or overly biologic, diagnostic or formulaic approach.

*Ruthellen:*  So what would happen in supervision when you would describe your sessions? How would they respond to what you said you were doing?

*Irv Yalom:*   Well at the end of the first year, Dr. Whitehorn called me into his office to give me a review of my first year's work. He said, "Dr. Yalom, all your supervisors agree that you would have a much better education if you'd spend more time trying to find out what they do know rather than focus on what they don't know."

I was trying to find out how I could do a better job, but none of it seemed right to me and anything that my own analyst was doing sure didn't seem right to me. As soon as I started residency, I began what would be a seven-hundred-hour psychoanalysis with a training analyst in the Baltimore-Washington analytic institute.

*Ruthellen:*   So what seemed not right?

*Irv Yalom:*   Well, just the coldness, the diagnostic viewpoint. You have to remember, though, that we were working in a place where residents in their very first year were exposed to the most difficult, untreatable patients, and asked to work with them therapeutically. That policy of assigning the most difficult patients to the beginning students is an unfortunate error that was common in most training programs.

*Ruthellen:* What you were coming most to prize was engagement with your patients.

*Irv Yalom:* I knew that in some unconscious way I was drawing from what I had learned from reading the great books in fiction. At that time my wife was getting her Ph.D. in comparative literature concentrating on Camus and Kafka and I was reading them very thoroughly and thought they had much to teach psychiatry. But there was such a gulf. Many of my peers and supervisors were unfamiliar with their work. John Whitehorn didn't know who Franz Kafka was. I gave him a book by Kafka and he read it but said he couldn't understand him. I knew that I drew from such literature in ways that I couldn't formulate very well, but I was approaching patients from a perspective of some greater wisdom than psychodynamics had to offer.

When I was a resident I read in my field voraciously. I read everything of Freud and Sullivan. I liked Horney very much. She was lucid and clear. And Erich Fromm, too. And Otto Rank. They brought some old world wisdom into their perspective, and they weren't reductionistic.

*Ruthellen:* So that leads to a question that I've been very interested in, which is that over the years, I've supervised and trained a great number of therapists. And so many of them have come to the work thinking that they could just be human and just bring themselves as human beings to other people and that this would be therapeutic for their patients. It's not. You know that too, because I'm sure you've had the same experience, supervising people who said well, I'm just going to come and be human.

So this, it seems to me, is a difficult thing to articulate. Your sensibility from the beginning—and what has developed over the years—was fundamentally a humanistic stance in regard to people, a shrugging off of anything that seemed reductionistic, or distancing, or categorical, but there was something else that was already in you that wasn't just a kind of "be nice to people" humanism. And I think you're getting a bit closer to it when you're talking about something like wisdom. I'm not sure that there really are words that you could apply because it just comes from inside of you, but there's something in your thinking that's different from, say, Rogerian humanism.

*Irv Yalom:* I drew from great thinkers. If a patient were talking about self-loathing, for example, I would have talked to them about Kafka's story of *Metamorphosis*.

That's quite typical of my approach—one of the things I want to convey is that great minds have dealt with these same problems. Right now I've been reading a great deal of Plato and Epicurus and I find that over and over again I bring many of their thoughts into my therapy sessions.

The idea that great thinkers have struggled with the same unanswerable questions is reassuring for a lot of people.

*Ruthellen:* What seems to them to be trivial problems are in fact great philosophical issues.

*Irv Yalom:* That's right. My reading of Epicurus has been very useful. His arguments about ways of dispelling the fear of death are enlightening. He spelled it out better than anybody ever has since then. So I draw upon his work when I am working with patients who have death terror.

*Ruthellen:* In your psychiatry residency, you began your education in philosophy and your entry point was through Bertrand Russell.

*Irv Yalom:* That's right, but then I began reading the other philosophers. Certainly the ones who had more to do with an existential approach, especially Camus and Sartre. And Kafka, and Stendhal, and more than anyone, Dostoevsky. These were great psychologists.

I think it is a great error to think that psychology began in the 19th century when the history of the field goes back 2000 years.

When I came to Stanford, I continued my education and audited many philosophy courses. Heidegger (I repeated that course a couple of times) and the background of phenomenology, and Nietzsche, Kierkegaard, Sartre and Plato and Aristotle. I've been a perpetual student.

One of my very good friends is a Norwegian philosopher named Dagfin Follesdal whose courses on Husserl and Heidegger I attended at Stanford. Afterward we taught a course together at Stanford that tried to combine philosophy and psychiatry.

The first few years of my career, I was very busy with the group therapy textbook, but underneath my thoughts about group therapy, there was a constant stream of thought about an existential therapy approach. These were parallel interests right from the beginning and they were quite separate.

*Ruthellen:* How do you think these concerns entered—or influenced—your interest in group therapy?

*Irv Yalom:* I don't think they did. I owe my interest in group therapy to Jerry Frank, whose therapy group I observed during my first year of residency. Of the various therapeutic approaches, the interpersonal approach was of most interest to me at Hopkins.

The ideas of Harry Stack Sullivan felt more cogent and important than some of the traditional psychoanalytic thought at that point and the whole idea of connection with people and the importance of peer relationships made powerful sense to me and seemed the key to the conduct of group therapy. I led therapy groups throughout my professional career and consider them a powerful, highly effective vehicle for change.

When I finished Hopkins, I went into the army and my major focus there was doing groups. I did groups of officers and officers' wives. I led all the in-patient groups every day as well as training an experiential group of psychiatric residents.

*Ruthellen:* From an interpersonal perspective?

*Irv Yalom:* Yes, all from an interpersonal standpoint. The way that I was leading groups then also took a more humanistic stance as I strove to become a participant observer. So I was leading the group, but I was experimenting with gradually becoming more self-revealing as a member of the group. This was one way I deviated from what I had learned from Jerry Frank. Jerry was never really involved as a person in the group. He was there to point out how people were communicating, and comment on problems, issues, and problems in communicating. He rarely focused upon himself nor did he reveal himself as a person.

*Ruthellen:* That's what I wanted to know about your growth as a therapist, or group therapist. Oftentimes one of the reasons that a relatively new therapist clings to theory, or to a concept, or to fancy words and catch phrases, especially in group therapy, is to deal with the

overwhelming complexity of all that's going
on. People cling to intellectual concepts to
keep their feet on the ground, to dispel an
uncomfortable sense of uncertainty.

So if I try to understand your development
as a therapist—first of all, there wasn't much
theory available about group therapy because
you hadn't yet written your book. Second of
all, Jerry wasn't there. He was in Baltimore
and you were in Hawaii. We didn't have
Internet, and email, and long distance calls
so you were really pretty much on your own.
You didn't have a co-therapist. I assume there
wasn't anybody there who would supervise
groups because it was all too new.

*Irv Yalom:*   No, none of that. It was all done by the seat
of my pants, which left me bathed in a tubful
of anxiety.

*Ruthellen:*   Well, that's what I want to know. How did you
manage yourself in this completely unfamiliar
environment with relatively unfamiliar technique, having thrown off the magical words
that psychiatrists use to protect themselves
from that anxiety? Here you are, you're working with officers, you're working with wives.
This isn't even a "psychiatric" population
and you're making groups available in lots

of different ways to lots of different kinds of people. So how did you think about what you were doing?

Again, you weren't just being "human" 'cause you couldn't go into that situation and just say "Hi, I'm Irv and we're just gonna sit here and talk." That's not what you were doing. You were holding some point of view, some way of thinking, and I know it's a really hard question.

*Irv Yalom:* It's hard to reconstruct, but first of all I should repeat that I was exposing myself to much uncertainty—that was necessary to experiment the way I did. Perhaps the extent to which one can try new ways is dependent upon how much anxiety one can carry. Well, I was pretty used to carrying anxiety because I had done it all my life. It was customary for me. Leading my first group of residents was not easy either. I knew I was being sized up and evaluated by professionals only a couple of years younger but I felt strongly I had something to teach them. I also had support from a couple of excellent colleagues in the army.

I also met several psychiatrists in practice in Honolulu. We started a discussion group that met once every week or every two weeks at one of their homes, and presented cases to one another, and that was very useful for me. I also started a psychiatrist's poker game there.

After his service in the Army, Yalom took an academic position at Stanford University, which he obtained, in part, on the strength of a glowing letter from his former teacher, John Whitehorn. This letter presciently predicted that Yalom would "become a leader in American psychiatry." Yalom remained at Stanford throughout his career, retiring from the faculty in 1994.

*Irv Yalom:* It was after the army in my early years at Stanford that I made a big jump in skills and knowledge about groups. I learned a great deal about groups with NTL (National Training Laboratory) and the whole T group and, later, encounter movement.

I attended, as a participant, an NTL lab at Lake Arrowhead. There were lots of short subjects (seminars and lectures) but the "T" group was the main feature. (The "T" stood for "training," that is, training in interpersonal relations.) The group I was in was led by a very savvy psychologist, Dorothy Semenow Garwood, who later became a long-term friend. She was a smart woman who, before entering psychology, had gotten a Ph.D.

in chemistry at the California Institute of Technology—the first such degree awarded to a woman.

I was floored when she started the group by saying, "I want us to stay entirely in the here and now." That was new for me. I'd been trying to do this implicitly in my groups, but here, without hesitation or self-consciousness, in the first sentence she uttered in the group, she made it explicit. I thought, "Are you crazy? How are we supposed to stay in the here and now when we don't know anything about each other? Zero. We have no history whatsoever."

Then some group members (there were about twelve in the group) started to talk about how uncomfortable they felt at the silence, and others said, "I'm not uncomfortable," and then others said they were really angry at her putting these restrictions on them. And soon we were exploring why one person was angry and nobody else was angry and why others were peaceful or uncomfortable or shy and, within 20 minutes, the group built a here-and-now history and was up and running.

That was a tremendously important experience, and I think when I returned to Stanford I immediately started being more explicit about the here-and-now in my therapy groups. I had already known that the time spent in the here-and-now was the most valuable time of the group therapy meetings. And something else important happened at Arrowhead, too. I was the only other psychiatrist in the hundred-person experience and had to take care of a guy who went psychotic in one of the groups. I had to go to the emergency room with him and eventually calm him down and made arrangements for a family member to take him home. That taught me more about the power of groups, that screening was essential and that poorly led groups can be dangerous.

And I continued to work at NTL as a faculty member and led groups at some of the labs and also led a week-long training of CEOs for another organization. I learned a great deal from NTL that I applied to group therapy.

*Ruthellen:* So when did you begin writing the group therapy text?

*Irv Yalom:* Well, it was already beginning to foment in my mind at that point, but I started writing in earnest during a year long NIMH fellowship in London at the Tavistock Clinic in 1967–68.

I had been co-director of the outpatient clinic at Stanford, and started a large group therapy program. That was my major responsibility.

Every single one of our twenty-four residents did a therapy group. So we had an enormous number of groups going in the clinic there and a waiting list of 50 to 60 patients to be put into groups. I had tremendous opportunities to set up clinical research. I also led each class of residents in a year-long experiential group.

*Ruthellen:* And you were supervising all these groups?

*Irv Yalom:* Well, I organized a team of supervisors from the clinical faculty. I found about ten excellent therapists with expertise in groups. Therapists in private practice were doing more group therapy in those days. So I had this cadre of high-quality supervisors. I also supervised several of the residents' groups. Every group got supervision for an hour for each group meeting they led. I also offered seminars in which I began to organize my thoughts that eventuated in my text.

Just as I had watched Jerry Frank's group, all the first year residents watched my therapy group the whole year. Then we met for an hour after each session. So I had a huge chunk of time to teach them. Today, residents in psychiatry don't get as much training in psychotherapy their whole three years as they got in that one year. And for the most part they get zero training in group therapy.

*Ruthellen:* And what you were bringing to your resident-students was your literary, person-centered, interpersonally-focused approach plus your new appreciation of the here-and-now.

*Irv Yalom:* Oh, yes, and very quickly after that, I began experimenting with being a participant of the group and disclosing more of myself. In keeping with that trend I decided to make the observation process more a part of the therapy group. So I experimented radically with the observational process. For example, for years I asked the group members and the observers to switch places at the end of the meeting, and the group members went into the observation room and they watched the rehash—the residents and myself talking about the group. That was a revelation.

*Ruthellen:* By self-disclosure, you mean self-disclosure in the here and now?

*Irv Yalom:* Yes. Nobody had ever permitted the group members to listen to the observers and group leader talking about the group. It transformed the observation process from an annoyance to the members to something valuable. They looked forward to observing the observers and, of course their responses to the observers became part of the group process in the next meeting.

Early on, too, I started writing summaries of each meeting that described what I thought I was doing, what I was pleased with in the group, why I was sorry I said certain things in the group, and so forth. And that was sent out weekly to the group. When I wrote my group therapy textbook, I had over a thousand of these summaries of groups, which provided all the clinical vignettes in the text.

*Ruthellen:* So your first major writing project was the group therapy text?

*Irv Yalom:* Right. Up to then I had only written articles in professional journals about various research projects in group therapy.

For example, in one project we interviewed all 30 dropouts from the clinic's therapy groups in one year to see why they dropped out. Then I started working with the durations of group meetings. Suppose we had a

12-hour group meeting or groups going away for weekends? I did projects on that. What about using a marathon group, all-weekend group, to kick-start people who are stuck in individual therapy? I did a project on that.

After a while, I grew very discouraged about empirical psychotherapy research. Let me tell you about an experience that ended my interest in outcome research. I was very interested, as of course was every researcher in the field, in psychotherapy outcome and different ways of measuring outcome. So I thought, "I'm going to really solve that problem in this way: I'm going to get large number of patients, have them interviewed in a semi-structured interview by an experienced clinician before they began therapy. This clinician would then interview them again three months later and then again six months later. I would videotape these three interviews.

And the interviewer for these patients was a highly skilled interviewer (Sid Bloch—who went on to have a stellar academic career in Australia) who would focus in each of the three interviews on the patient's view of the major problems in his/her life and the degree of distress or dysfunction associated with each of these problems.

Okay, then I got a group of therapists in the area, each with 15 to 20 years of experience, the best psychiatrists and psychologists all around the Stanford geographic area. They volunteered to come in and spend a least half a day watching all three tapes (that is, the first interview, three months and then six months later) and rate each of the major problems on various scores of severity. Surely, I thought, that would give us a reliable rating. No simplistic paper and pencil tests of self-ratings, no rating by inexperienced research assistants—these were the top clinicians—the cream of the cream.

But, alas, there was zero order of correlation among them. There were tremendous disagreements about whether the patient improved or not, and what the major problems were. It was unbelievable. And, of course, it was never published. No journal at that time would publish totally negative results. That was not only the last research I did, but the last time I really trusted outcome research. And it was about then that I started planning my book, *Existential Psychotherapy*.

As I said, I wrote the group therapy book on my sabbatical fellowship in London. First I wrote two chapters that were really middle chapters based on research data, including much of the vast group literature. It's really, really exhaustive. I was a very thorough scholar at that point.

So I wrote these two chapters and one of them was on the selection of patients for group therapy and the second one was on the composition of groups because I was in this unusual position of having 50 people on a waiting list. I could assign any of these people, according to some pre-determined characteristic, to any of a number of groups. I could put ten people of one kind in a group, ten people of another kind into another group and then observe these groups for the number of drop-outs, the cohesiveness of the group. I learned much during these first years about selection of patients and group composition.

These two chapters were extremely scholarly and thorough. And they were deadly. Then I was visited in London by my chairman, Dave Hamburg, who informed me that Stanford had awarded me tenure.

And it was at that moment that I decided to write in a different way, to communicate in a reader-friendly manner. Even now, five editions later, those two chapters that I wrote for the tenure committee stick out like a sore thumb.

*Ruthellen:* And they're still there?

*Irv Yalom:* Oh yes, they're still there because the topic is important. But they're dull and opaque and, even though I've worked hard on them in all four subsequent revisions, I've never been able to make them engaging. The rest of the book I wrote in a narrative way. Lots and lots of stories, one after the other. Short one-paragraph stories.

*Ruthellen:* This was a completely new style in writing textbooks in the field?

*Irv Yalom:* That's right and I cannot tell you how often I've heard students tell me that they really like this book because it reads like a novel or they're willing to put up with some dry riff on theory because they know there's a little story waiting in the next corner or something like that.

*Ruthellen:* This just came naturally to you?

*Irv Yalom:* Absolutely.

*Ruthellen:*   You didn't say "I'm going to do a radical thing here"? What you said to yourself is "I'm just going to try to communicate with people."

*Irv Yalom:*   Exactly. I just wanted to communicate. Clarity and liveliness were all-important. I had a cardinal rule for myself: Never write a sentence that you don't understand yourself.

And Yalom did communicate—to millions of therapists and students of psychotherapy all over the world. These people found that learning from his storied format, stories framed by the wisdom of philosophy and great literature, taught them what academic or textbook presentations could not—how to "be" with patients.

This then brings us to the writing of his first book, *The Theory and Practice of Group Psychotherapy*, a book now in its fifth edition, a kind of secular Bible in the mental health literature, translated into seventeen languages. Over 38 years, its message has endured. This is the moment when, as I said before, I first encountered the writing of Irvin Yalom, and found the model for how I wanted to be as a therapist—fully present, direct, and humane. Millions of other therapists have been similarly influenced.

In the next four chapters, I trace the most significant ideas of Yalom's worldview and the evolution of his thinking as his career progresses.

# 2

# The Dilemmas of Existence
# and Beyond

In his group therapy textbook, *The Theory and Practice of Group Psychotherapy*, Yalom attempts to detail how group psychotherapy heals. Given the diversity of types of therapy groups, what factors are common to the healing that takes place in all? Yalom organized the book around a set of therapeutic factors, each illustrated by stories that show how therapy groups can, among other possibilities for healing, instill hope in the members and provide opportunities for altruism, for the positive change that comes from giving something of value to someone else. Therapy groups also offer a setting for imparting information and learning new skills for communicating with others. Above all, group therapy, when conducted well, gives patients an opportunity to learn about how they are with other people, what impact they have and what they need from others.

Yalom believes that patients have symptoms because something is awry in their relationships with people in their lives and they are unable to get what they need from others. The best way to help them with their difficulties is to understand their way of being with others and then to help them make changes so that their relationships become more satisfying and meaningful. So, for example, depression may be understood interpersonally as a problem in passivity and isolation, or as an inability to express anger toward others or as overwhelming fears of separation.

In group therapy, one doesn't have to *ask* patients what is troubled in their relationships—as the group process unfolds, this will be become apparent to all. One central task of the therapist is to create a cohesive group where people are committed to the work of the group. Then, the group becomes a miniature version of each person's social world and learning occurs through an intensive focus on what is taking place in the moment, in the here and now. To do this well, therapists must be available to openly discuss their own experience of patients as well as to be sensitive to their reactions to them and to one another. This takes enormous skill, tact and empathy—and Yalom offers many instances from his own experience to help therapists develop these.

Over the years, keeping this textbook up to date in its many editions presented a challenge for Yalom and he continued not only to read the evolving research literature about groups but also to maintain detailed notes about his own groups so the material would always be fresh.[2] He also expanded the kinds of groups that he worked with so that he would continue to learn about the processes that occur in the wide range of possible groups. And what he learned from groups with bereaved parents, AIDS patients, convicted murders, corporate CEOs, sexual deviants and cancer patients (among others) also enlarged his understanding of the universal aspects of the human condition.

With the success of his first book and his academic career assured, Yalom was then free to follow his more pervasive interests and invent—or at least, explicate—the field of Existential Psychotherapy. After reading philosophy and literature for many more years, Yalom took on the Herculean task of trying to integrate this body of thought with academic psychotherapy. Ten years in the writing, *Existential Psychotherapy* describes having human encounters at the deepest levels of awareness of the human condition. Existential psychotherapy is not a "school" of therapy like cognitive behaviorism or psychoanalysis. Rather, it represents a way of thinking about human experience that can be—or perhaps should be—integrated into all therapies. Although in this book he is primarily attentive to how therapists of all persuasions can become more attentive to the universal problems of life, he is also meditating on the timeless and intractable issues of the "ultimate concerns": death, freedom, isolation, and meaning. The book is both a guide for therapists and itself a form of existential therapy. Anyone who reads it comes away profoundly moved and wiser, as though they have just spent many hours talking to someone willing to walk with them unflinchingly through life's deepest and most vexing problems.

Yalom links the work of existential psychotherapy to classical forms of therapy by telling what is one of my favorite stories from the corpus of his work, a story I have repeated many times. He tells of taking part in an Armenian cooking class where the teacher, who did not speak English well, taught mainly by demonstration. As hard as he tried, he could never quite make his dishes taste as good as hers did. He decided to observe his teacher more carefully and in one lesson noted that when she finished her preparation she handed her dish to her servant who took it into the kitchen to place into the oven. He observed the servant and was astounded, and edified, to note that that before throwing the dish in the oven, the servant threw in handfuls of various spices that struck her fancy. These "throw-ins" he likened to the interactions that therapists have with their patients that, because they are not conceptualized within their theoretical "recipe," go unnoticed. Perhaps, however, these off-the-record extras are the critical ingredients. And perhaps theses throw-ins refer to the shared issues of human existence.

Where, he asks, in the early pages of *Existential Psychotherapy*, in the lexicon of psychiatry are terms such as "choice," "responsibility," "mortality," or "purpose in life"? These are issues that all therapists know to be central concerns of patients. His aim in this book was to shift the focus away from diagnosable "symptoms" and place these ultimate concerns at the center of the therapeutic gaze.

Yalom defines the stance of the existential therapist with such terms as authenticity and compassion, but his central metaphor, which continues throughout his work, is that of being a "fellow traveler." We all, whether in the role of patients or therapists or just as a human being, must come to terms with our eventual death, with our aloneness in the universe, with finding meaning in life and with recognizing our freedom and taking responsibility for the lives we lead. The wise therapist recognizes that these are issues with which we must struggle together; the therapist is only privileged in the sense of being able, one hopes, to talk honestly about what these concerns entail. The therapist, in Yalom's portrayal, is Everyman.

These major existential concerns are not new, of course, and Yalom suggests that it is reassuring to know that an unbroken stream of philosophers, theologians and poets since the beginning of recorded history have wrestled with them. Yalom's contribution is to organize and synthesize them and then to see how they may be expressed in the therapy consulting room—and in straightforward language. But these are not issues that are easy for anyone to talk about. It is more comfortable to talk with a patient about medication for depression than the search for meaning in life.

An awareness of ultimate freedom is always connected to dread. While freedom is a cherished value in Western culture, if we look honestly at the extent of our freedom, we see the absence of external structure. We live in a universe without inherent design in which we are free to author our own lives. Life is groundless and we are responsible for our choices.

Indeed, the therapeutic enterprise can be conceived of as one in which the client actively increases his or her freedom: freedom from destructive habits or from self-limiting beliefs, just to name a few. However, when using the term "freedom," Yalom is not referring to political liberty, or to the greater range of possibilities in life that come from increasing one's psychological awareness. Instead, he addresses a profound and awesome freedom that carries with it terrifying responsibility, the kind of freedom people fear so much that they enlist dictators, masters and gods to remove the burden from them. He is fond of, and often quotes, Erich Fromm's term, "the lust for submission."

Ultimately, we are "responsible" for what we experience in and of the world. Yalom sees responsibility as inextricably linked to freedom because we are responsible for the sense that we make of our world and for all of our actions and our failures to act. An appreciation of responsibility in this sense is very unsettling. Everything in the universe is contingent. Our most cherished ideas, our most noble truths, the bedrock of our convictions are all undermined by this awareness. Similarly, we bear the burden of knowing that we are responsible, that we are, in Sartre's terms "the uncontested author," of everything we have experienced.

The complement to responsibility is our "will." Yalom acknowledges this concept has waned of late in the social sciences, replaced by terms such as "motivation." But he rejects that term because to claim a person's behavior is explained (i.e., caused) by a certain motivation is to deny that person's ultimate responsibility for his or her actions. "Motivations may influence but cannot replace will; the individual still has the option of behaving or not behaving in a certain fashion.[3]" People are responsible for their decisions and to abrogate such responsibility is to live inauthentically, in what Sartre has called "bad faith."

Because of the dread of our ultimate freedom, people erect a plethora of defenses, some of which give rise to psychopathology. The work of therapy is very much about the assumption of responsibility for one's experience. Yalom sees one of the major tasks of the therapist to be helping patients see how their decisions and actions have helped create the situations in which they find themselves (often repeatedly). Borrowing a phrase from Erich Fromm, Yalom maintains that there is no escape from existential freedom.

Another ultimate concern is that of existential isolation, our aloneness in the universe, which, though assuaged by connections to other human beings, yet remains. We enter and leave the world alone and while we are alive, must always manage the tension between our wish for contact with others and our knowledge of our aloneness.

Aloneness is different from loneliness, which is also a ubiquitous issue in therapy. Loneliness results from social, geographic, and cultural factors that support the breakdown of intimacy. Or people may lack social skills or have personality styles inimical to intimacy. These are amply addressed in group therapy. But *existential* isolation cuts even deeper; it is a more basic isolation that is riveted to existence and refers *to an unbridgeable gulf between oneself and others*. It is most commonly experienced in the recognition, a common theme among poets and writers, that one's death is always solitary. But many people are in touch with their dread of existential isolation when they recognize the terror of feeling that there may be moments when no one in the world is thinking of them. Or walking alone on a deserted beach in another country, one may be struck with the dread: "Right at this moment, no one knows where I am." If one is not being thought about by someone else, is one still real?

In working with people who have lost their spouse, Yalom was struck not only by their loneliness but the accompanying despair at living an unobserved life—of having no one who knows what time they come home, go to bed, or woke up. Many individuals continue a highly unsatisfying relationship precisely because they crave a life witness, a buffer against the experience of existential isolation.

The professional literature regarding the therapist-patient relationship abounds with discussions of encounter, genuineness, accurate empathy, positive unconditional regard, and "I-thou" relating. The sense of deep connection, while it does not "solve" the problem of existential isolation, nevertheless provides solace. Yalom tells about one of the members of his cancer group who said, "I know we are each ships passing in the dark and each of us is a lonely ship but still it is mighty comforting to see the bobbing lights of the other nearby boats." Still, we are ultimately alone. Even a therapist cannot change that. Yalom comments that an important milestone in therapy is the patient's realization that, "there is a point beyond which they [the therapist] can offer nothing more. In therapy, as in life, there is an inescapable substrate of lonely work and lonely existence.[4]"

All humans must find some meaning in life although none is absolute and none is given to us. We create our own world and have to answer for ourselves why we live and how we shall live. One of our major life tasks is to invent a purpose in life sturdy enough to support a life; often, we then deny our personal authorship of this purpose and it may seem to us that it was "out there" waiting for us. Our ongoing search for substantial purpose-providing life structures often throws us into a crisis. More individuals seek therapy because of concerns about purpose in life than therapists often realize. The complaints take many different forms: "I have no passion for anything," "Why am I living? Surely life must have some deeper significance." "I feel so empty—just trying to get ahead makes me feel so pointless, so useless." "Even now at the age of fifty I still don't know what I want to do when I grow up."

In a lecture to the American Psychiatric Association, Yalom quoted a story that stayed with him for a long time, a story Allen Wheelis[5] told about a moment with his dog, Monty. The story was this:

If then I bend over and pick up a stick, he is instantly before me. The great thing has now happened. He has a mission . . . It never occurs to him to evaluate the mission. His dedication is solely to its fulfillment. He runs or swims any distance, over or through any obstacle, to get that stick.

And, having got it, he brings it back: for his

mission is not simply to get it but to return it. Yet,
as he approaches me, he moves more slowly. He
wants to give it to me and give closure to his task,
yet he hates to have done with his mission, to again
be in the position of waiting.

For him as for me, it is necessary to be in the
service of something beyond the self. Until I am
ready he must wait. *He is lucky to have me to throw
his stick.* I am waiting for God to throw mine. Have
been waiting a long time. Who knows when, if ever,
he will again turn his attention to me, and allow
me, as I allow Monty, my mood of mission?

Who among us has not had the wish, Yalom asks: *if
only someone would throw me* MY *stick.* "How reassuring
to know that somewhere there exists a true purpose-in-
life rather than only the *sense* of purpose-in-life. How
much more comforting is the religious solution to the
problem of meaning than the more rational but bleak
message sent us by nature, a message that reminds us
of our miniscule place in the cosmos and in the great
chain of being.[6]"

To Yalom, people's life-purpose projects take on a
deeper, more powerful significance if directed to something or someone outside themselves—the love of a cause,
the creative process, the love of others or a divine essence.
But this is a question that cannot be pursued directly.
Rather, Yalom believes, a sense of meaning emerges from
plunging into an enlarging, fulfilling, self-transcending
endeavor. The work of the therapist is to identify and

help to remove the obstacles to such engagement. If one is authentically immersed in the river of life, then the question drifts away.

Overshadowing all these ultimate concerns, the awareness of death, of our inevitable demise, is the most painful and difficult. We strive to find meaning in the context of our existential aloneness and take responsibility for the choices that we make within our freedom to choose, yet one day we will cease to be. And we live our lives with that awareness in the shadow. Death is always the distant thunder at our picnic, however much we may wish to deny it. Of the four ultimate concerns, death is the one that Yalom returned to in *Staring at the Sun*, which he thought of as his last book, relying on the Greek philosophers to help him to advise his readers about how to overcome the fear of death. In this book, he addresses his audience—everyone—directly, no longer filtering his message through the psychotherapy profession.

He writes: "It's not easy to live every moment wholly aware of death. It's like trying to stare the sun in the face: you can stand only so much of it. Because we cannot live frozen in fear, we generate methods to soften death's terror. We assuage it by projecting ourselves into the future through our children, or by trying to growing rich and famous, or by developing compulsive behaviors, or by fostering an impregnable belief in an ultimate rescuer.[7]" Our fear of death is a profound dread of non-being, "the impossibility of further possibility," as Hidegger put it. And fears of death can lurk disguised behind many symptoms as well. Writing as a man confronting his own eventual death, he argues in this book that confronting death allows us to live fuller, richer, more compassionate lives.

Everything fades. This is the sad existential truth. Life is seriously linear and irreversible. As Yalom presents it, it is this knowledge that can lead us to take stock of ourselves and ask how we can live our lives as fully as possible. Drawing especially on Heidegger, Yalom argues for the importance of living mindfully and purposefully, aware of one's possibilities and limits in a context of absolute freedom and choosing. Death, in this view, enriches life.

Yalom is particularly taken by Tolstoy's account of *The Death of Ivan Illych*, which he takes up in both *Existential Psychotherapy* and *Staring at the Sun*. Ivan Illych, a self-involved, self-satisfied, pompous bureaucrat is dying in pain when he realizes that he is dying badly because he has lived badly. "Maybe I did not live as I ought to have done," it suddenly occurred to him. "But how could that be, when I did everything properly?[8]" Ivan Illych's realization of the impoverishment of his life leads him, in the last days of his life, to relate more authentically and empathically to his family, thus redeeming his life at the very end. Yalom views this as a parable of all of our lives. Are we living as authentically and meaningfully as possible?

During the 1970s, before and during the writing of *Existential Psychotherapy*, Yalom chose to work with groups of terminally ill cancer patients and groups of bereaved people to get closer to these existential issues. His major teachers were always his patients. And what he learned from them affirmed what he learned from Tolstoy and the philosophers. People with terminal illnesses reported living more intensely, more passionately, more deliberately. Indeed, the awareness of the nearness of death led them to richer and more authentic experience. They described the experience of reprioritizing their life values, of saying "no" to the things that are unimportant, of turning full attention to loving those around them, to the rhythms of the earth and its changing seasons. He understood more deeply how the inevitability of death can enhance life. While he details all the ways in which people (and therapists) live in denial of death, perhaps looking it in the face is what we need to live life fully. In *Staring at the Sun* he refers to instances of confrontation with death as "awakening experiences."

People rarely bring their anxieties about death to therapists. Rather, it is masked behind complex defenses that Yalom sensitively reveals. People can camouflage their fears of death behind a belief that one's specialness will somehow override the dread decree. Again, drawing on Tolstoy, Yalom quotes Ivan Illych:

> In the depth of his heart he knew he was dying, but not only was he not accustomed to the thought, he simply did not and could not grasp it.
>
> The syllogism he had learnt from Kiezewetter's Logic, "Caius is a man, men are mortal, therefore Caius is mortal," had always seemed to him correct as applied to Caius, but certainly not as applied to himself. That Caius—man in the abstract—was mortal, was perfectly correct, but he was not Caius, not an abstract man, but a creature quite,

quite separate from all others. He had been little
Vanya, with a mamma and a papa . . . What did
Caius know of the smell of that striped leather ball
Vanya had been so fond of? Had Caius kissed his
mother's hand like that . . . ? Had Caius been in
love like that? Could Caius preside at a session as
he did? Caius really was mortal, and it was right
for him to die, but for me, little Vanya, Ivan Illych,
with all my thoughts and emotions, it's altogether
a different matter. It cannot be that I ought to die.
That would be too terrible.⁹"

What psychiatrists might simply label as narcissism or
entitlement, in Yalom's view may actually be subterfuge
for the belief that specialness is an antidote for death.
Similarly, workaholism or preoccupation with getting
ahead, with preparing for the future, amassing material
goods, growing larger, more powerful, more eminent can
be compulsive ways of unconsciously trying to ensure immortality. The illusion of immortality sponsored by many
religious systems is one of the major defensive systems
against the dread of death.

A second denial system is belief in an ultimate rescuer.
People may imagine their rescuer to be human or divine,
but the belief is in someone who is watching over them in
an indifferent world. Yalom is an avowedly non-religious
thinker. To him, belief in the supernatural is a way of
avoiding confrontation with painful facts of existence.

In 2002, he was astonished to be awarded the Pfister
Prize by the psychology and religion committee of the

American Psychiatric Association.[10] When he first learned of the prize, he thought, "Religion? Me? There must be some mistake." He wrote to the committee and asked, "Are you sure? You know I regard myself as a practicing atheist?"

Yalom's early religious experience in his family's orthodox Jewish synagogue was cloaked in rigid, unyielding authoritarianism that he found highly distasteful.

Later, he grew to believe that the religious and the scientific world views were incompatible and he resonated with Schopenhauer's metaphor of religion being like a glow worm that was visible only in the darkness of ignorance. Yalom was drawn to atheistic existentialism, philosophers such as Nietzsche, Sartre, Heidegger and Schopenhauer and to the Presocratics and the Stoics. "I very much want to contain the divine spark, I crave to be part of the sacred, to exist everlastingly, to rejoin those I've lost—I wish these things very much but I know these wishes do not alter or constitute reality," he said in his Pfister lecture, applying his teachings in *Existential Psychotherapy* to himself.

Yalom regards the ubiquity of religious belief as evidence of the ubiquity of existence anxiety. People create gods to comfort them from the pain of the ultimate concerns and Yalom cites Xenophanes, the Presocratic free-thinker, who wrote 2500 years ago, "If Lion could think, their Gods would have a mane and roar.[11]" Yalom believes that humans created God to assuage their existential dilemmas, but he is nevertheless respectful of people's need for religious belief. The therapist's first task is always to be caring for one's patient and this involves being empathic with a person's belief system.

In *Staring at the Sun,* he tells the story of his encounter with a young Orthodox Jewish rabbi who was interested in becoming a psychotherapist and had come because he was wrestling with the contradiction between his own devout religious beliefs and Yalom's writings. But the rabbi was challenging him, doubtful that Yalom could live meaningfully without faith. The conversation between them gave Yalom a chance to explicate clearly his capacity to live a moral, meaningful life without the supernatural. Yalom told the rabbi, ". . . meaning, wisdom, morality, living well—are *not* dependent on a belief in God. I dedicate myself to helping others heal and grow. I live a moral life. I feel compassion for those about me. I live in a loving relationship with my family and friends. I don't need religion to supply a moral compass.[12]"

If one is to engage deeply with patients, fundamental questions about existence and meaning will emerge, yet many therapists shy away from such discussions. Yalom's efforts to engage existential concerns from the vantage point of the therapeutic consulting room inevitably link his work to the project of theologians and religious leaders who similarly are asked to embody or clarify a worldview that makes life meaningful and possible in the face of death. Psychiatry has historically been loath to take up issues of meaning and existence and Yalom has provided a guide for talking genuinely about what theologians might call the human soul.

Yalom accepts the transience of life; his worldview

has no need of something beyond. One need not fear death if one has the sense of having fulfilled one's potential—up until the last moments. It is never too late to live authentically. "How staggeringly lucky I am to be here, alive, and luxuriating in the pleasure of sheer being![13]" he writes—offering his own reflections on his life (and his own death anxiety) as a model for his readers.

In two powerful stories in his book, *Momma and the Meaning of Life*, he demonstrates the anguished journey of a therapist trying to work with a patient who is terminally ill and another who is mired in intractable grief over the loss of her husband. The route is filled with pain, for both patient and therapist, as each have to encounter the sometimes unbearable realities of mortality. The deliverance is in engagement, intense human engagement in which the therapist dares to meet the patient in the nucleus of the pain, dares to stare together at the sun.

One of Yalom's central premises is that "confronting death need not result in despair that strips away all purpose in life. On the contrary, it can be an awakening experience to a fuller life. *Though the physicality of life destroys us, the idea of death saves us.*[14]" From his earlier formal research on bereaved patients, he demonstrated that following confrontation with the death of a loved one and the profound loss that follows, patients not only returned to previous levels of functioning but went beyond. And this is vividly apparent in many of his psychotherapy stories as well. Living with awareness of death helps people to rearrange their life priorities by trivializing life's trivia, and to live more fully.

All things in life are transient and death is inevitable. In *Staring at the Sun*, Yalom proposes the idea of "rippling" as a way of coping with these immutable facts. "Rippling refers to the fact that each of us creates—without our conscious intent or knowledge—concentric circles of influence that may affect others for years, generations. . . . The idea that we can leave something of ourselves, even beyond our knowing, offers a potent answer to those who claim that meaninglessness inevitably flows from one's finiteness and transiency.[15]" While our *personal* identity, our sense of who we are or even the way in which others have known us, will finally disappear, nevertheless we may leave behind something that passes to another person and will in turn be passed on in ways we cannot imagine or predict. The notion of rippling thus satisfies, at least to some extent, the heart-wrenching longing to project oneself into the future. Eventually we will not be remembered, but "something of each of us persists even though it may be unknown or imperceptible to us."

Summing up the existential therapeutic position twenty-five years after he wrote his classic, influential text, Yalom acknowledges that psychological distress "issues *not only* from our biological genetic substrate (a psychopharmacologic model), *not only* from our struggle with suppressed instinctual strivings (a Freudian position), *not only* from our internalized significant adults who may be uncaring, unloving, neurotic (an object relations position), *not only* from disordered forms of thinking (a cognitive-behavioral position), *not only* from shards of forgotten traumatic memories, nor from current life crises involving one's career and relationship with significant others, *but also—but also*—from a confrontation with our existence.[16]"

The therapeutic approach in *Existential Psychotherapy* does not suggest that therapy be limited to or even focused on a discussion of these ultimate concerns, although the alert therapist aims not to shy away from them or change the subject. Rather, Yalom's premise is that awareness of these givens of existence fundamentally changes the relationship between therapist and patient to that of *fellow travelers.* From this vantage point, even labels of patient/therapist, client/counselor, analysand/analyst become inappropriate to the nature of the relationship. If there were such language, he would advocate some term that abolishes distinctions between "them" (the afflicted) and "us" (the healers). "*We are all in this together* and there is no therapist and no person immune to the inherent tragedies of existence."

"Sometimes I feel a deep sorrow for the underlying fragility of the human condition which begets our gullibility and our powerful need to believe. Sometimes I fear the future because of the dangers that irrational belief creates for our species. It is supernatural belief, not absence of belief, that may destroy us. We need only look to the past to trace out the huge swaths of destruction that unyielding conviction has caused. Or look to contemporary struggles where conflicting and unyielding fundamentalist belief systems threaten millions. I love Nietzsche's aphorism that *it is not the courage of one's convictions that matters but the courage to change one's convictions.* There are times when I feel (but keep to myself) sorrow as I consider the amount of an individual's life that can be spent in bondage to obsessive-compulsive behavior, and to practices of prolonged meditation or excessive preoccupation with ritualistic practice. What is lost is some part of human freedom, creativity and growth.

"In his four noble truths, the Buddha taught that life is suffering, that suffering originates from craving and attachment, and that suffering can be eliminated by detachment from craving through meditative practice. Schopenhauer took a similar position—that the will is insatiable and that as soon as one impulse is satisfied we enjoy only a moment of satiation which is instantly replaced by boredom until another desire seizes us. To me, these views feel unnecessarily pessimistic. I appreciate the suffering in human existence but I never experience that suffering as so overwhelming that it demands the sacrifice of life. I much prefer a Nietzschian life-celebratory, life engagement, *amor fati* (love your fate) perspective. My work with individuals facing death has taught me that death anxiety is directly proportional to the amount of each person's 'unlived life.' Those individuals who feel they have lived their lives richly, have fulfilled their potential and their destiny, experience less panic in the face of death.[17]"

# 3

# Fellow Travelers

A stark confrontation with the ultimate concerns of life leads to a recognition of the primacy of connectedness in human life. As he matured as a therapist, Yalom realized more and more that what is central to psychotherapy is the relationship between therapist and patient. But noticing that the texture of the relationship is crucial to therapeutic change was not new. Many had recognized that it is the *relationship* that heals. For decades, therapists had been writing about the importance of empathy, unconditional positive regard or the therapeutic alliance. But they had written in abstract terms. Yalom wanted to go beyond this and to detail what a therapist might actually *do* in the therapy hour. He imagined a student asking, "If I were a fly on the wall in your office, what would I see happen during your therapy hours?"

To respond to this urgent imagined question, Yalom turned to story, drawing on his long interest in literature and his wish to emulate the great writers. His first effort in this direction was a creative and utterly original venture—to write about therapy *with* one of his patients. When Ginny Elkins, a gifted creative writer entered his

office in 1974, unable to afford his fee to help overcome
her writing block, he decided to try an unusual experiment. He suggested that, in lieu of payment, she write a
free flowing, uncensored summary of each therapy hour.
Yalom proposed that he do exactly the same. Each week
his secretary would type out their summaries and they
would read each other's notes every few months.

   In devising this plan, Yalom was hoping not only to
unblock his patient's writing and to encourage her to
express herself more freely in therapy but also to break
his professional shackles and to liberate his own voice.
It was an exercise in therapist transparency because he
intended to write uncensored notes in which he would
disclose all that he experienced during the hour.

   These notes, published in edited form as *Everyday
Gets a Little Closer: A Twice-Told Tale* were edifying for
all therapists. The story of Ginny and Yalom's developing relationship in their therapy sessions is a Rashomon
experience. Although they had shared each hour, their
experiences were very different. For one thing, they
valued very different parts of the session. She absorbed
none of what he considered to be his elegant and brilliant
interpretations. But she did value the small personal acts
that he barely noticed: his complimenting her appearance,
chuckling at her satire, teasing her when she role-played,
or teaching her how to relax. The book is an exercise in
post-modern realism. What we think is happening is only
one version of reality and woe to the therapist who loses
awareness that the patient may be having a completely
different experience of the interaction.

Beyond this, though, is the naked honesty of Yalom's self-scrutiny in this book. He felt that Ginny had so idealized him, had placed him on such an elevated pedestal that a true meeting between them was not possible. Therefore, in his notes he deliberately attempted to reveal the very human feelings and experiences he had—his frustrations, his irritations, his insomnia, his vanity. For whom is he acting in the therapy session, he wonders? He *likes* having Ginny in love with him. He asks himself if he is secretly and silently seducing her with his wise pronouncements. Are they having a highly sublimated affair? He wonders about his rescue fantasies, his wish to shape her to his own image of her. These are dangerous questions, ones that perhaps torment all therapists in the dead of night, but questions that are rarely spoken, let alone written about for all to see. There is always love and narcissism, idealization and contempt, unrealizable hope and unfathomable dread on both sides of the therapeutic encounter. Irrationality exists in the people in both chairs. At the same time, Yalom struggled with the confounding paradox that his irrational needs and wishes were also the energy behind the good work they did together. Recognizing these feelings, examining and controlling, rather than denying them, is what makes therapy heal. And, in the same vein of utter openness, Yalom unblinkingly acknowledges one of the most painful truths about psychotherapy: the therapist is always far more important to the patient than the patient to the therapist. How does one manage a fully genuine relationship in light of this unchangeable fact? The patient has just one therapist, the therapist many patients.

Yalom had reached a profound understanding of the essence of psychotherapy, and his later work on therapy technique enlarged on these insights. He summarized it again in *Staring at the Sun*: "I strive for connectedness above all else. To that end, I am resolved to act in good faith: no uniforms or costumes; no parading of a phalanx of diplomas, professional degrees, and awards; no pretense of knowledge I do not possess; no denial that existential dilemmas strike home for me as well; no refusal to answer questions; no hiding behind my role; and, finally, no concealing my own humanness and my own vulnerabilities.[18]"

At the end of their work together, Ginny's writing was unfrozen, her other symptoms and difficulties abated, and Yalom was also freed of his professional fetters and ready to venture into a new arena. He had accepted that psychotherapy was an "art" that transcended scientific principles and objective analysis and set out then to write the ineffable: what actually occurs in the richness and depth of the therapeutic encounter.

To do this, he began to integrate his literary and philosophical interests with his psychiatric and medical ones in the form of narratives of his experiences with his patients. Rather than using stories to illustrate therapeutic and theoretical principles, he now aimed to move the story to the center and allow the theory of practice to emerge from it. He took as models the philosophers who decided that much of the deep experience they wished to depict was better done through literature than through formal philosophical prose: Camus, Sartre, Unamuno,

Kierkegaard, Nietzsche, Ortega Y Gassett, and Simone de Beauvoir. And he emulated Richard Lindner's classic stories of psychotherapy in *The Fifty-Minute Hour*, published over forty years before.

These accounts could be read as case histories or short stories, and they would detail the interaction between himself and his patients. Unlike case histories that others had written, though, these were not stories that were to tell of the strangeness of the abnormal, but rather the humanity of the meeting between—what became a central motif in Yalom's work—*fellow travelers*. Yalom was not writing to document his success or demonstrate his cleverness as a therapist. Rather, he meant to show how his experiences as a therapist who was fully *with* his patients, even when he made mistakes, led to the therapeutic balm of connection.

Although he meant *Love's Executioner* to be a collection of teaching tales to be used in psychotherapy training programs, it spent many weeks on the bestseller list and was translated into twenty languages (where it also reached bestseller lists in many countries). The brilliance of these ten stories was that they induced the reader to enter into the relationship Yalom created with each of his patients and to be moved in a human way by the universal concerns they discussed. Part fictionalized to preserve the anonymity of his patients and for literary effect, these stories distilled the essence of people in their existential struggles with life. Existence pain, he called it. Destiny pain. We, like the people whom Yalom creates in his book, suffer from knowing that our deepest wants can never be fulfilled—our wishes not to age or die, for the return of lost loved ones, for eternal love, protection and significance. The book spoke to masses of readers and profoundly altered the ways in which therapists approached their work (and perhaps also the ways in which patients approached their therapists). Many people who were neither therapists nor patients but just humans dealing with the ordinary suffering of life, felt their lives enriched, perhaps even healed, by these stories.

In the opening story of the same title, Yalom begins "I hate to be love's executioner . . ." But he goes on to tell the story of wrestling with the demons of his patient's obsessive and hopeless unrequited love. Trying every rational argument, every possible persuasion, he is ultimately defeated. Love is too powerful for his reason to conquer, but the genuineness and the compassion of his encounter with his love-struck patient sounds the theme of the book. He invites the reader to *be* the fly on the wall, to join him and his patients as they together untangle the mysteries of human psychic pain.

From the beginning of his psychiatric career, Yalom kept a journal of illuminating therapy events—clarifying moments of insight, instances that captured the essence of a state of being. For Elva, an elderly woman traumatized by having her purse snatched, Yalom penetrates through to her belief in her specialness and her inability to let go of her departed husband who she, at a very deep level, believed would continue to protect her. In this story, Yalom shows us how the need for an ultimate rescuer may masquerade in the dailiness of life.

Carlos, the focus of one of the most powerful chapters, is dying of cancer yet has increased his preoccupation with having sex with as many women as possible. In a powerful exchange that seems almost like a chess game, Yalom risks being cruel in undermining Carlos' denial of his impending death. But Yalom's insistence that he reflect on how he has been living his life leads Carlos to astonishing change in his last months. And as he lies dying, he thanks his therapist for having saved his life.

As Yalom the therapist guides his patients toward recognition of their inescapable freedom to choose, Yalom the storyteller illuminates how all people are involved in constructing the prisons that they feel limit them. Through willing and deciding, taking responsibility for their choices, people change.

*Love's Executioner*, of course, offers no easy solutions to these implacable dilemmas. Yalom is well aware that there is always much that is unknowable about the other person no matter how deep or meaningful the encounter. We must learn to stay connected to one another in uncertainty. He shows us how the therapist gropes toward the patient with improvisation and intuition. "The heart of psychotherapy is a caring, deeply human meeting between two people, one (generally but not always, the patient) more troubled than the other.[19]" Both are exposed to the same existential issues of meaning, isolation, freedom and death. Yalom's premise is that knowing about the human condition is better than not knowing—even if this means relinquishing comforting illusions that, in Yalom's view, ultimately weaken the human spirit. And as a fellow traveler, he undertakes the difficult and painful journey with his patients—and his readers.

# 4

# The Dialogue Between
# Psychotherapy and Philosophy

The more he read philosophy, the more Yalom was
intrigued by the links between philosophical reflection
and the healing that takes place in psychotherapy. Perhaps
the philosophers were covert therapists. Perhaps the wise
therapist may have offered something to soothe the tra-
vails of the philosopher. And what *is* the journey toward
existential knowledge and wisdom?

A tale from Herman Hesse made a profound impression on Yalom. The tale was this:

Joseph and Dion, two renowned healers, lived
in Biblical times. Though both were highly effective, they worked in different ways. The younger
healer, Joseph, healed through quiet, inspired
listening. Pilgrims trusted Joseph. Suffering and
anxiety poured into his ears vanished like water
on the desert sand and penitents left his presence
emptied and calmed. On the other hand, Dion, the
older healer, actively confronted those who sought

his help. He divined their unconfessed sins. He was a great judge, chastiser, scolder, rectifier and healed through active intervention. Treating the penitents as children, he gave advice, punished by assigning penance, ordered pilgrimages and marriages, compelled enemies to make up.

The two healers never met and worked as rivals for many years until the younger healer, Joseph, grew spiritually ill, fell into dark despair, and was assailed with ideas of self destruction. Unable to heal himself with his own therapeutic methods, he set out on a journey to seek help from Dion.

On his pilgrimage, Joseph rested one evening at an oasis where he fell into a conversation with an older traveler to whom he described the purpose and goal of his pilgrimage. The older man replied, "Oh, this is indeed a miracle. I am the very man you seek." Without hesitation Dion invited his younger, despairing rival into his home where they lived and worked together for many years, first with Joseph a student, later a full colleague. Years later the older man fell ill and on his death bed called Joseph to him. "I have a great secret to tell you," he said, "—a secret that I have long kept. Do you remember that night we met on the oasis and you told me you were on your way to see me?"

The younger man replied, "Of course, I remember. How could I forget that night? It was the turning point of my entire life."

The dying Dion took Joseph's hand and said,

"My secret is that I, too, was in despair and on the night of our meeting I was traveling to seek help from you.[20]"

Yalom found this story compelling as a tale about giving and receiving help, about honesty and duplicity, and about the relationship between the healer and patient. The younger healer was nurtured and mentored while the older healer obtained a disciple from whom he received filial love, respect, and salve for his isolation. But Yalom wondered if perhaps the *real* therapy occurred at the deathbed scene when these two men acknowledged that they were both simply human, all too human. And what would have happened if this were the beginning of a conversation between them rather than the end? What would it be like, for example, if a great philosopher, Nietzsche (with whose writings Yalom was in intense conversation) were to consult a great therapist of his time—Josef Breuer, under whose guidance Freud was led to psychoanalysis? Could they, like the wise men in Hesse's story, heal one another? Could Nietzsche have invented psychotherapy based on his philosophical ideas? Yalom took from André Gide the idea that *Fiction is history that might have happened.* If history had been just a bit different, perhaps Nietzsche might have actually encountered Breuer.

Yalom was perhaps more drawn to Nietzsche than any of the philosophers he was avidly reading for he found in Nietzsche the fundamental particles of psychotherapy. Yalom understood Nietzsche, through his writings, as someone who wished to be a healer. From his viewpoint,

Nietzsche's idea of the death of God was an opportunity
to create a new set of values, values based not on supernatural illusions, but upon human experience. Like the
ideal therapist, Nietzsche's *Übermensch* (or *superman* or
*overman*) overflows with power and wisdom and offers it
freely to others. He is a life affirmer, one who loves his fate
and says "yes" to life. Nietzsche's overman is one who, if
offered the opportunity to live life precisely the same way,
again and again and for all eternity, is able to say, "Yes, yes,
give it to me. I'll take that life and I'll live it again in precisely the same way." Yalom saw in Nietzsche's philosophy
a movement toward an interior, self-actualizing process,
toward the possibility of realizing one's own potential.
Nietzsche's instruction for the necessary inner work was,
"Become who you are." What could be a more succinct
statement of the goal of existential psychotherapy?

Yalom found Nietzsche's ability to stare unflinchingly
at the truth, to break illusion, remarkable. "That which
does not kill me makes me stronger" was one of his major
teachings. To become enlightened, one must face down
the terror of death and to plunge into one's own dying
many times while still alive—much as Yalom concluded
in his own earlier writings. Indeed, Nietzsche *could* have
invented psychotherapy.

Yalom believes that Freud was influenced by Nietzsche's
work. When the Gestapo forced him to leave Vienna
and to leave much of his library behind, Freud took with
him to London a complete set of Nietzsche's writings,
which Otto Rank had given him. The minutes of the
Psychoanalytic Society in Vienna show that two entire

meetings in 1908 were devoted to Nietzsche. In these minutes, Freud acknowledged that Nietzsche's intuitional method had reached insights amazingly similar to those reached through the laborious systematic efforts of psychoanalysis, including the significance of abreaction and repression, and a view of illness as an excessive sensitivity to the vicissitudes of life. But the budding field of psychotherapy followed Freud's lead and ignored Nietzsche's contributions. Thus, part of Yalom's interest was to restore Nietzsche to what he felt was his rightful place in the history of psychotherapy. He aimed to do this not through academic argument—but through fiction.

There were, therefore, many roots to Yalom's readiness to make a full leap into fiction. He still thought of himself as a teacher of psychotherapy—but one now working through the medium of the novel. Keeping himself grounded in all that he knew about psychotherapy, he fictionalized Nietzsche, Breuer—and even Freud—and set them in relationship to one another. Then, like all good novelists, he let the drama between them unfold. To set the stage, Yalom returned to a question that he had explored in *Love's Executioner*—the problem of obsessional love.

In *When Nietzsche Wept*, Yalom creates the premise that an admirer and friend of Nietzsche consults Breuer on behalf of her friend and asks Breuer to surreptitiously find a way to treat Nietzsche's melancholy, his suicidal thoughts, and his tormenting headaches. Readers are let in on secrets carefully guarded by both men. They have a similar secret: each is hopelessly, painfully, and obsessively in love with a (different) woman who is unavailable to them. Finding no other way to engage—and thereby treat—Nietzsche, Breuer discloses his secret to Nietzsche and asks for his help. As a physician, I'll treat your body, Breuer proposes, in exchange for you ministering to my anguished despair. Thus the "therapeutic" relationship begins to unfold. The focus of the novel is on the gradual creation of an authentic relationship between these men, which is ultimately redemptive to both.

"I don't know *why* to live. I don't know *how* to live," Breuer tells Nietzsche. "Save me. Practice on me. I believe in the healing value of talking. Simply to review my life with an informed mind like yours—that's what I want. That cannot fail to help me." Although the relationship begins duplicitously, Breuer is lured by the power of the therapeutic process and cannot resist becoming a genuine patient.

What kind of therapist would Nietzsche have been? Yalom depicts Nietzsche as a resolute and uncompromising therapist. He would have expected his clients to face the truth about themselves and their "situation" in existence. In the novel, all of Nietzsche's responses as a therapist derive from his published writings. Nietzsche invents a number of methods to lay bare the existential roots of Breuer's despair. The crucial moment comes when they together visit the grave of Breuer's parents and Nietzsche tells Breuer that his love obsession is a way of avoiding his fears of oblivion and of death. Have you chosen your life? Have you consummated your life? Nietzsche asks him. And Breuer says no, he has not but is powerless to change his commitments. Nietzsche then proposes his central thought experiment—and here Yalom has Nietzsche advance the core idea of what was to become *Thus Spake Zarathustra,* the idea of eternal recurrence. Can you live each moment so that you would be willing to live it over and over again forever?

What if, some day or night, a demon were to steal after you into your loneliest loneliness and say to you: "This life as you now live it and have lived it, you will have to live once more and innumerable times more; and there will be nothing new in it, but every pain and every joy and every thought and sigh and everything unutterably small or great in your life will have to return to you, all in the same succession and sequence—even this spider and this moonlight between the trees, and even this moment and I myself. The eternal hourglass of existence is turned upside down again and again, and you with it, speck of dust!" Would you not throw yourself down and gnash your teeth and curse the demon who spoke thus? Or have you once experienced a tremendous moment when you would have answered him: "You are a god and never have I heard anything more divine." If this thought gained possession of you, it would change you as you are, or perhaps crush you.[21]

The idea of living your identical life again and again for all eternity can be jarring, a sort of existential shock therapy. It serves as a sobering thought experiment, increasing your awareness that this life, your *only* life, should be lived well and fully, accumulating as few regrets as possible. (Many years later, in *The Schopenhauer Cure* and *Staring at the Sun*, Yalom described his use of this thought experiment in psychotherapy practice.) In the novel, Nietzsche tells Breuer that as long as he clings to his sense of duty as a curtain to hide behind, he can never know his freedom. *Amor fati* (love your fate) Nietzsche instructs: in other words, *create the fate that you can love*. Eventually, in the novel, Breuer does just this.

What would Nietzsche have needed from a therapeutic relationship? Surely not insight. Freud had said that Nietzsche was a man who had more insight about himself than any man who ever lived. But Nietzsche experienced himself as desperately isolated. What Nietzsche needed was a therapeutic encounter, a meaningful relationship, which Yalom provided him in the shape of Breuer. Through their talks and the growing openness and depth of their relationship, Nietzsche ultimately experiences a fully human touch. What leads Nietzsche to weep is the recognition that he and Breuer have become friends.

> Here and there on earth we may encounter a kind of confirmation of love in which this possessive craving of two people for each other gives way to a new desire—a shared higher thirst for an ideal above them. But who knows such love? Who has experienced it? Its right name is friendship.[22]

"A shared thirst for an ideal above them . . . its right name is friendship." In his novel, though, Yalom goes beyond this and suggests that the right name for this particular kind of authentic relationship may be psychotherapy.

*When Nietzsche Wept* secured Yalom's place as a fiction writer. Reviewers compared him to Freud. The book won many prizes and was translated into 24 languages, appeared on nearly as many best seller lists, and sold over two million copies. It brought both Nietzsche and psychotherapy into the hearts of people all over the world and led them to think about their own encounters with destiny.

Having portrayed the origins of psychotherapy in the philosophy of Nietzsche, Yalom continued to explore through fiction the dialogue between psychotherapy and philosophy. What would Schopenhauer, the philosopher of pessimism, have to say about Yalom's approach to healing? In *The Schopenhauer Cure*, Yalom imagines that a contemporary philosopher, a Schopenhauer clone, enters one of his therapy groups. This patient, Phillip, isolated, formerly addicted to meaningless sexual conquests, has hopes of becoming a philosophical counselor, a sort of existential therapist, using Schopenhauer's ideas to heal others. Yalom, in the guise of his alter ego therapist, Julius, persuades Phillip to enter his therapy group where, to Julius' amazement, this distant, unfeeling man engages the other members of the group with his (Schopenhauer's) philosophical ideas. Soon Julius and Philip, using very different therapeutic approaches, are competing for the hearts and minds of the group members.

In the novel, Julius, recently diagnosed with a terminal cancer, is also confronting his own death:

Julius knew the life-and-death homilies as well as anyone. He agreed with the Stoics, who said, "As soon as we are born we begin to die," and with Epicurus, who reasoned, "Where I am, death is not and where death is, I am not. Hence why fear death?" As a physician and a psychiatrist, he had murmured these very consolations into the ears of the dying.[23]

But what does it mean for a real person to confront death? Can Julius live each day fully and meaningfully—of course he can—and how does he do this? Part of what Julius finds most sustaining to him is his work with this group. And Phillip becomes perhaps his last great challenge.

Like Schopenhauer, Philip has armored himself in a philosophy of renunciation that teaches that attachments add to life's inevitable suffering. Self-reliance and getting off "this cycle of endless desires" are his antidote. Yalom has Phillip declare to the group:

"The more attachments one has, the more burdensome life becomes and the more suffering one experiences when one is separated from these attachments. Schopenhauer and Buddhism both hold that one must release oneself from attachments . . .[24]"

To which Julius responds,

"I come in on that in the opposite way—attachments, and plenty of them, are the indispensable
ingredients of a full life and to avoid attachments
because of anticipated suffering is a sure recipe to
being only partially alive.[25]"

In *The Schopenhauer Cure*, Yalom intersperses a psychobiography of Schopenhauer and traces the origins of
his pessimism and misanthropy. Schopenhauer lived a life
of isolation. In his most famous parable, he depicted man-
kind as two porcupines who huddle together for enough
warmth to keep them from freezing but then are pricked
by each other's quills and move apart. Schopenhauer
strove to generate warmth from within and to neither
give to nor receive it from others. Schopenhauer saw
life as an endless cycle of wanting, satisfaction, boredom
and then wanting again. Desires endlessly plague us and
cannot be fulfilled.

Phillip, in the novel, tormented by compulsive sexual
desire, had adopted Schopenhauer's solution as a way
of living.

"Schopenhauer made me aware that we are
doomed to turn endlessly on the wheel of will: we
desire something, we acquire it, we enjoy a brief
moment of satiation, which rapidly fades into boredom which then, without fail, is followed by the

next 'I want.' There is no exit by way of appeasing desire—one has to leap off the wheel completely. That's what Schopenhauer did and that's what I've done."

And what does it mean to leap off the wheel completely, one of the other group members asks Phillip?

"It means to escape from willing entirely. It means to fully accept that our innermost nature is an unappeasable striving, that this suffering is programmed into us from the beginning, and that we are doomed by our very nature. It means that we must first comprehend the essential nothingness of this world of illusion and then set about finding a way to deny the will. We have to aim, as all the great artists have, at dwelling in the pure world of platonic ideas. Some do this through art, some through religious asceticism. Schopenhauer did it by avoiding the world of desire, by communion with the great minds of history, and by esthetic contemplation—he played the flute an hour or two every morning. It means that one must become observer as well as actor. One must recognize the life force that exists in all of nature, that manifests itself through each person's individual existence and that will ultimately reclaim that force when the individual no longer exists as a physical entity.

"I've followed his model closely—my primary relationships are with great thinkers whom I read daily. I avoid cluttering my mind with everydayness, and I have a daily contemplative practice through chess or listening to music—[26]"

While finding a way to come to terms with his own dread of death, Julius, with the aid of the group members, must persuade Phillip/Schopenhauer of the importance of human relationship to meaning in life. And they must do this by engaging him, something no one ever succeeded in doing with the historical Schopenhauer.

The conversations among the characters in the group and with Julius and Phillip again feature the themes of mortality, despair and the difficulties of intimacy, and the characters debate Schopenhauer's ideas about them. Schopenhauer believed that if one were to go to any cemetery, knock on the tombstones, and ask the spirits dwelling there if they'd like to live again every one of them would emphatically refuse. While Phillip had been cured of his sexual compulsion by reading Schopenhauer, the group's task, as one of the characters in the novel phrases it, is to save him from Schopenhauer's cure.

The novel, then, becomes a debate between the life-denying, life-is-suffering philosophy of Schopenhauer and the life-affirming *amor fati* position of Nietszche, with which Yalom is strongly allied. But Yalom also admires much in Schopenhauer and sees him (along with Nietzsche) as having been a major influence on Freud.

Toward the end of the novel, Julius/Yalom tells Phillip:

"I don't disagree with much that you and Schopenhauer have said about the tragedy of the human
condition. Where you go east and I go west is when
we turn to the question of *what to do about it.* How
shall we live? How to face our mortality? How to
live with the knowledge that we are simply life
forms, thrown into an indifferent universe, with
no preordained purpose? . . . You know, when I
first received my diagnosis and was in a state of
panic, I opened *Thus Spoke Zarathustra* and was
both calmed and inspired—especially from his life
celebratory comment that we should live life in
such a manner that we'd say 'yes' if we were offered
the opportunity to live our life again and again in
precisely the same manner."

"How did that relieve you?" asked Philip.

"I looked at my life and felt that I had lived it
right—no regrets from *inside* though, of course, I
hated the *outside* events that took my wife from me.
It helped me decide how I should live my remaining
days—I should continue doing exactly what had
always offered me satisfaction and meaning.[27]"

Phillip resists worldly connections, but the group, led
by Julius' example, struggles mightily to engage him. As
the group enables Phillip to learn about the value of human relationship, Yalom also teaches his therapist-readers
about how to conduct group therapy. Phillip had lived a

life without love but within the "Yalom cure," he finds his way to experience the flooding warmth of human, caring touch just as Julius' (unfeared) death ends the group. The title of the book is a double entendre: "The Schopenhauer Cure" refers both to the cure that Schopenhauer provides and to the cure that Schopenhauer needs.

The beginnings of this novel sprang from Yalom's recognition that Nietzsche and Schopenhauer started with the same data, the same observations about the human condition. Yet the two philosophers had diametrically different responses; Nietzsche embraced life while Schopenhauer negated it. The reason for this divergence, Yalom concluded, resided in Schopenhauer's significant personality disorder, which he explored in psychobiographical chapters that he interspersed in the novel.

*The Schopenhauer Cure* is the one volume in which Yalom combined his existential and his group therapy interests. It was Yalom's intention that *The Schopenhauer Cure* also serve as a companion volume to his group therapy textbook, and the fifth edition of *The Theory and Practice of Group Psychotherapy* is studded with cross references to pages of *The Schopenhauer Cure* that provide illustrations of a number of group therapy principles.

While both *When Nietzsche Wept* and *The Schopenhauer Cure* lucidly introduce the reader to the complex thought of major philosophers and also demonstrate techniques of psychotherapy, they both offer the same conclusion: Whatever salvation there might be in the tragedy of the human condition evolves from a recognition

of our status as fellow travelers, of being in the futility
and passion of life together, and in genuinely engaging
one another in loving relationships.

# 5

# The Promise of Psychotherapy

A vivid demonstration that it is the therapeutic relationship that heals is also the central theme of *Lying
on the Couch,* a playful novel, at times comic and satiric,
that pushes to the limit the questions of the nature of the
therapeutic encounter. The operation of genuineness and
authenticity in actual therapeutic encounters is less clear
than the empirical research studies would make it seem.
"Picture the psychotherapy hour. A therapist and patient
converse. How can we determine if the therapist is being
'genuine' or authentic? In real time what does that mean?
For example, does 'genuineness' entail sharing one's feelings openly in therapy? Feelings about patients? About
the therapist's own life? Own problems? Should therapists
form deep attachments to patients? Love their patients?
Profit personally from the therapy they offer?[28]"

Yalom was fascinated by an experiment undertaken by
Sandor Ferenczi (1873–1933), a Hungarian psychoanalyst
who was a member of Freud's inner psychoanalytic circle
and perhaps Freud's closest professional and personal
confidant. What would it be like, Ferenczi wondered, to
have "mutual analysis," where he analyzed a patient one

hour and the patient analyzed him the next? Ferenczi attempted this with one of his patients but the experiment failed, shipwrecked on the treacherous analytic reefs of confidentiality and the problem of who should pay whom. Ultimately he grew discouraged and abandoned the experiment. His disappointed patient believed Ferenczi was unwilling to continue because he feared having to acknowledge that he was in love with her. Ferenczi held a contrary opinion: that he was unwilling to express the fact that he hated her.

Yalom was drawn to Ferenczi's experiment because he had himself always explored the possibilities of greater openness about the therapeutic process. In his work with groups, both inpatient and outpatient, he had often had "rehash" sessions where the student observers and therapists would discuss the group and share their own reactions while being observed by the patients. And in the days before economic considerations drove therapy practice, he had sometimes used a teaching in which he and several students offered therapy to a single patient and encouraged the patient to observe their discussion after the session. The point was to make the therapy process—and the inner experience of the therapist—fully transparent.

With his long experience in therapy groups, Yalom was intensely aware of the mandate for therapists to be interactive and transparent. Group leaders are lightning rods for so many powerful feelings that they must thoroughly work through their relationships with the group members. And the leaders' behavior models the norms of the group. Transparency, he believes, is no less important in individual therapy where therapists must relate deeply to patients and must be willing to be open about the mechanisms of therapy and about their own here-and-now feelings. Disclosure by the therapist always facilitates therapy. "Very frequently in my practice I see patients who have had some prior unsatisfactory therapy. Over and again I have heard the same complaint: the therapist was too impersonal, too uninvolved, too wooden. I have almost never heard a patient complain of their therapist for being too open, too interactive, or too personal (aside of course from sexually exploitative therapists.),[29]" Yalom said.

But what are the limits and boundaries of such disclosure? "Is it possible for a relationship to be genuine and yet at the same time sharply and formally limited? Does not the strict time limit, the formality, and the exchange of money corrode the genuineness of the relationship? Is the therapist a friend? Is there love between therapist and patient? Does therapeutic love include touching or holding? What are, what should be, the sexual, social, business, financial boundaries of a therapeutic relationship?"

"These are not only crucial and complex contemporary concerns, they are also highly inflammatory ones. There have been so many lawsuits, so many cases of reported abuse by therapists (and priests, teachers, physicians, police officers, employers, supervisors, gurus—by anyone involved in a power differential) that to discuss boundaries in a comic irreverent novel felt distinctly risky. I attempted to maintain a balanced perspective—on the

one hand to address the alarming incidence of abuse suf-
fered by patients and, on the other hand, to confront an
equally alarming development—the legalistic backlash that
threatens the very fabric of the therapy relationship.

"What is one to think, for example, of articles in professional journals which seriously propose that *all* therapy
hours be videotaped with a continuously running security
patrol camera to protect the patient from therapist sexual
abuse (and to protect the therapist from false charges)?
Therapists are advised to practice *defensive* psychotherapy.
The legal profession has so invaded the intimacy of the
therapy hour that many don't stop to consider the extent
to which a security TV camera would destroy the heart
of the therapy enterprise. Therapists are taught to write
progress notes in charts as though a hostile attorney were
reading them.[30]"

Yalom's desire in *Lying on the Couch* was to explore
therapist-patient boundary issues in all their complexity:
the risks and temptations, the desires of the therapist, the
modes of avoiding pitfalls, the dangers to the exploited
patient. Therapy is always a two-person drama and Yalom
wanted to explore the deep subjective experience of each
participant without rushing to brand or to lynch. Hence
*Lying on the Couch* explores many controversial questions,
even, for example, the delicate one of whether, if the
relationship is a genuine one, there may be a legitimate
role for sexual energy (not sexual behavior) in successful
therapy. It was a risky venture. It was also Yalom's only
foray into pure fiction—no philosophers to form the basis
of his characters, no patients mildly disguised. In *Lying*

*on the Couch*, he gave himself license to invent therapists, patients and other characters—still with some desire to teach about psychotherapy. This is the most intricately plotted and least overtly pedagogical of his works, but any student of psychotherapy finds much to challenge his or her thinking about the process.

The double-entendre of the title, *Lying on the Couch*, (which, by the way, is untranslatable into any other language) raises the question of lying within therapy. Overt lying is part of everyday business in forensic psychiatry or in any situation where some third party—the law, an employer, an insurance company, or a spouse—intrudes into the therapy situation. But in the traditional therapy relationship where patients pursue greater self-understanding and personal growth, lying takes far more subtle forms—concealment, exaggeration, omission, or distortion. Everyone conceals. Often they conceal vital facts about their personal lives that they are ashamed to reveal. Equally often they conceal their strong feelings in the moment—toward the others present in group therapy, or toward the therapist in individual therapy. Envy, attraction, fear and repulsion are kept hidden. Memory is unreliable and therapists often find it difficult to distinguish fiction from truth. The injunction to be always truthful, never to lie, is thus fraught with confusion and dilemmas.

Ernest Lash, the protagonist of *Lying on the Couch* attempts to rerun Ferenczi's experiment. Though he does not reveal as much as Ferenczi, he does resolve to be absolutely honest in his interactions with his next patient. Unfortunately, though, his next patient is a woman who, angry at him because she thinks he has encouraged her husband to leave her, is duplicitous and revenge-driven—a patient in disguise, who comes to seduce him in hopes of then suing him for malpractice.

The novel opens with a prologue in which Seymour Trotter, an eminent psychiatrist, is charged with flagrant sexual misconduct with a young female patient, and is being interviewed by the young Ernest Lash, a member of a hospital medical ethics committee. Seymour Trotter is a wounded healer, part erring, part wizard. His story is meant as a cautionary tale, a dark backdrop against which the rest of the novel will be played out. In the novel are many therapists, each representing a way of thinking about therapy and a way of being a therapist. The pomposity and politics of analytic institutes are satirized, the very hubris of the profession lambasted. Above all, there is great uncertainty and many pitfalls in the effort to create genuineness in the relationship between therapist and patient.

"You have to be bold and creative enough to fashion a new therapy for each patient," the erring therapist, Seymour Trotter, in *Lying on the Couch* tells Ernest Lash. One must abandon all artificial "technique." And diagnosis becomes more useless the better one gets to know a patient. Successful therapy rests on two people making contact. But how far can one go with this? Clearly, Trotter had gone too far. In powerful prose, the fully realized characters of *Lying on the Couch* explore the thorny question of the boundaries of psychotherapy.

The novel's hero, Ernest Lash, strives to be a man—and

a therapist—of integrity. Despite his lust, his bumbling, his struggles with his primitive appetites, he remains totally committed to his patients and to his vision of the continuing possibility of human growth. And through the novel, which is filled with plot twists and surprises, Yalom affirms that therapist authenticity will ultimately be redemptive even under the worst circumstances.

Surveying the contemporary therapeutic world when he emerged from the years of writing *Lying on the Couch*, Yalom found psychotherapy to be under assault from managed care companies that demanded fast symptom relief. In most psychiatry training programs, psychotherapy was—and still is—being taught less and less and rarely in terms of the subtleties that Yalom was working so hard to explicate in his writings. Psychiatry had become the science of dispensing medication. In psychology and social work, cognitive behavioral approaches that offer manualized treatment for highly specific disorders, prevail. Incrementally, despite research showing that it is the therapeutic relationship that is the dominant healing aspect of psychotherapy, attention to the nature and creation of such a relationship is being pushed aside.

Yalom began to view his work as serving future generations who may wonder what psychotherapy was like in the good old days when deeper forms of healing were possible. His storied accounts offer detailed, readable, even delightful renderings of what takes place behind the closed doors of the consulting room. From the short vignettes in the textbook on group therapy to the full account of the sessions of a long-term therapy group in

*The Schopenhauer Cure*, readers are invited to be a fly on the wall and learn from the master. Yalom is equally revealing of his individual therapy work in the two short story case books and in *Lying on the Couch*.

Chagrined at seeing the life being squeezed out of psychotherapy as it was becoming more mechanized and less human and intimate, Yalom next decided to write a highly accessible guide for therapists, both novice and seasoned, titled appropriately *The Gift of Therapy*. In this 2002 book, he distills his wisdom in 85 one-to-two-page "lessons"—illustrated, of course, with stories.

Noting that the shelf life of eminent theorists in mental health has grown short, he begins by paying homage to Karen Horney whose book *Neurosis and Human Growth* had profoundly influenced him. He takes from her the notion that the human being has an inbuilt propensity toward self-realization and if obstacles are removed, the individual will develop into a mature, fully realized adult, just as an acorn will develop into an oak tree. Thus, the work of the psychotherapist can be understood as removing obstacles to growth, a core idea of his own approach.

He teaches that the therapeutic venture is always spontaneous, creative and uncertain. Again he stresses his life-affirming vision of the tragic view of life. Engage the patient, be supportive, he exhorts. Try to look out the patients' window and see the world through their eyes. One of his most memorable (to me) stories concerns a young woman complaining of being locked in a long bitter struggle with her nay-saying father. Yearning for some form of reconciliation, for a new, fresh beginning to their relationship, she looked forward to her father's driving her to college—a time when she would be alone with him for several hours. But the long-anticipated trip proved a disaster: her father behaved true to form by grousing at length about the ugly, garbage-littered creek by the side of the road. She, on the other hand, saw no litter whatsoever in the beautiful, rustic unspoiled stream. She could find no way to respond and eventually, lapsing into silence, they spent the remainder of the trip looking away from one another.

Later, she made the same trip alone and was astounded to note that there were *two* streams—one on each side of the road. "This time I was the driver," she said sadly, "and the stream I saw through my window on the driver's side was just as ugly and polluted as my father had described it.[31]" But, by the time she had learned to look out her father's window, it was too late—her father was dead and buried.

Yalom reminds his readers to *keep in mind that patients view the therapy hours in very different ways from therapists.* Again and again, therapists, even highly experienced ones, are surprised to rediscover this phenomenon when their patients describe an intense emotional reaction about the previous hour that the therapist cannot recall. It is extraordinarily difficult to really know what the other feels; far too often we project our own feelings onto the other.

Therapists don't have to have the same experience as patients to be empathic. They might try to follow the maxim that "I am human and let nothing human be alien

to me." This requires that therapists be open to that part
of themselves that corresponds to any deed or fantasy
offered by patients, no matter how heinous, violent, lust-
ful, or sadistic.

Yalom believes that the therapist's most valuable
instrument is his or her own self and, therefore, the
personal exploration that can only be conducted in
one's own therapy is necessary. Only through this route
can therapists become aware of their own blind spots
and dark sides and thus become able to empathize with
the extensive range of human wishes and impulses. A
personal therapy experience also permits the student
therapist to experience the therapeutic process from the
patient's seat: the tendency to idealize the therapist, the
yearning for dependency, the gratitude toward a caring
and attentive listener, the power granted to the therapist.
Psychotherapy is a psychologically demanding enterprise,
and therapists must develop the awareness and inner
strength to cope with the many occupational hazards of
psychotherapy. And therapists can only benefit from re-
entering therapy at many stages of life. Self knowledge is
not achieved once and for all.

Far from being a detached "expert," Yalom advises therapists to "let the patient matter to you[32]" and to disclose
(tactfully) the impact patients have on you. "Acknowledge
your mistakes and work with them. These help build an
intimate and trusting relationship. Be ready to go where
the patient goes and to devise a unique therapy for each
patient.[33]"

When he delves into the nitty-gritty of *doing* therapy,

the key concept is again the "here and now." What is happening in the interpersonal space between patient and
therapist, right here, right now? In Yalom's view, people
fall into despair because of their inability to form and
maintain enduring and gratifying interpersonal relationships. Psychotherapy based on his model is directed toward
removing the obstacles to satisfying relationships. Therapy
is a social microcosm in the sense that sooner or later, if
the therapy is not highly structured, the interpersonal
problems of the patient will manifest themselves in the
here-and-now of the therapy relationship. If, in life, the
patient is demanding or fearful or arrogant or self-effacing
or seductive or controlling or judgmental or maladaptive
interpersonally in any other way, then these traits will
be displayed in living color in the here-and-now of the
therapy hour. The therapist need only be alert to what is
happening in the interaction with the patient and to try
to find the analogues to what the patient reports to be
his or her difficulties in outside relationships. In order to
fully access the here and now, therapists have to access
their own feelings and to use these as a barometer of what
is happening in the interaction. If the therapist is bored,
there is something the patient is doing to induce that
boredom. Perhaps the patient fears intimacy or is silently
rageful toward the therapist. Only by acknowledging his
or her feelings in the immediacy of the interaction can
the therapist access what is being enacted by the patient.
To do this well, the therapist must both have deep self-
knowledge and the skill to give feedback tactfully and
kindly, to avoid accusation of the patient and above all, to

be ready when necessary to acknowledge his or her own contribution to the problematic interaction.

In Yalom's approach to (individual) therapy, what occurs in the here-and-now between therapist and patient is the site of the deepest and most fruitful therapeutic work. It is the task of the therapist to maintain focus on what is transpiring in this space between them, in the relationship as it develops. Yalom advocates a simple check-in to bring this relationship to the center of attention, asking, for example, such questions as: "How are you and I doing today?" "Are there feelings about me you took home from the last session?" "I've noticed a real shift in the session today. At first it seemed we were very distant and in the past twenty minutes, I felt much closer. Was your experience the same? What enabled us to get closer then?"

Don't make decisions for patients, Yalom instructs his readers. It is folly to think that the therapist can ever have all the necessary information. Therapy is aimed toward removing roadblocks to purposeful living and helping patients assume responsibility for their actions, not providing solutions.

Dreams are a very important access road to the inner life of patients. They comment on the therapy relationship, on existential experiences, on unconscious fantasies and contain metaphors for the deepest aspects of the person. Yalom, in preparing patients for therapy, tells them of the importance of dreams, asking them even to keep a pad and pencil next to the bed to record them. He recounts the following story in *The Gift of Therapy*, to demonstrate how dreams can enliven and direct the therapy. One of his patients had the following dream:

> I was on the porch of my home looking through the window at my father sitting at his desk. I went inside and asked him for gas money for my car. He reached into his pocket and as he handed me a lot of bills he pointed to my purse. I opened my wallet and it already was crammed with money. Then I said that my gas tank was empty and he went outside to my car and pointed to the gas gauge which said, "full.[34]"

In his analysis of this dream, Yalom points out that "the major theme in this dream was emptiness versus fullness. The patient wanted something from her father (and from me since the room in the dream closely resembled the configuration of my office) but she couldn't figure out what she wanted. She asked for money and gasoline but her wallet was already stuffed with money and her gas tank was full. The dream depicted her pervasive sense of emptiness, as well as her belief that I had the power to fill her up if she could only discover the right question to ask. Hence she persisted in craving something from me—compliments, doting, special treatment, birthday presents—all the while knowing she was off the mark. My task in therapy was to redirect her attention—away from gaining supplies from another towards the richness of her own inner resources.[35]"

Some of his advice to therapists continues in the radical

vein of questioning authority with which he began his
career. Avoid diagnosis, he counsels. Some day the idea
that people could be formulated into neat categories in
what he calls "the DSM–IV Chinese restaurant menu
format" will appear ludicrous to mental health professionals. And he finds protocol driven treatments with
a standard format for each week "an abomination." For
Yalom, therapy involves constructing a unique therapy for
each unique patient and his recognition that this project of
construction is the therapy itself. That is, as therapist and
patient grope uncertainly toward one another, stumbling
against one another's limitations, trying to deeply find one
another beyond their defenses, that is the therapy itself.
In effect, Yalom was teaching years ago what the new
schools of relational psychoanalysis are just discovering.
What is healing about psychotherapy is what occurs in
the space *between* therapist and patient.

In part, Yalom wrote *The Gift of Therapy* in order
to counter the social forces that aim to standardize
psychotherapy and confine it within a pseudo-scientific
framework. He writes, "The concept of the EVT (empirically validated therapy) has had enormous recent
impact—so far, all negative—on the field of psychotherapy.
Only therapies that have been empirically validated—in
actuality, this means brief cognitive-behavioral therapy
(CBT)—are authorized by many managed care providers.
Graduate psychology schools granting masters and doctor-
ate degrees are reshaping their curricula to concentrate
upon the teaching of the EVTs; licensing examinations
make certain that psychologists are properly imbued

with the knowledge of EVT superiority; and major federal psychotherapy research funding agencies smile with particular favor upon EVT research.

"All these developments create dissonance for many expert senior clinicians who are daily exposed to managed care administrators insisting upon use of EVTs. Senior clinicians see an apparent avalanche of scientific evidence proving that their own approach is far less effective than that offered by junior (and inexpensive) therapists delivering manualized CBT in astoundingly brief periods of time. In their guts they know this is wrong, they suspect the presence of smoke and mirrors, but have no evidentially-based reply and generally they have pulled in their horns and tried to go about their work hoping for the nightmare to pass.[36]"

Yalom calls attention to other work that challenges the premises of empirically validated treatment as well as some of the findings that reflect experimental treatments under conditions that never actually occur in real treatment situations. EVT research makes many false assumptions: that patients have only one definable symptom they can report at the onset of therapy, that long term problems can yield to brief therapy, that the elements of effective therapy can be separated out one from one another, and that a written systematic procedural manual can permit minimally trained individuals to deliver psychotherapy effectively.

Further, Yalom makes the point that "*nonvalidated* therapies are not *invalidated* therapies.[37]" It is nearly impossible to *validate* the effects of "therapies which rely on an intimate (unscripted) therapist-patient relationship forged in genuineness and focusing on the here-and-now as it spontaneously evolves."

It is clear from Yalom's writing that being a psychotherapist and doing psychotherapy is richly rewarding in countless ways. But there are nevertheless occupational hazards. "Psychotherapy is a demanding vocation and the successful therapist must be able to tolerate the isolation, anxiety, and frustration that are inevitable in the work.[38]" He counsels early-career therapists to pay close attention to having fulfilling relationships with people in their lives:

"The therapist's world view is itself isolating. Seasoned therapists view relationships differently, they sometimes lose patience with social ritual and bureaucracy, they cannot abide the fleeting shallow encounters and small talk of many social gatherings. While traveling, some therapists avoid contact with others or they conceal their profession because they are put off by the public's distorted responses toward them. They are weary not only of being irrationally feared or devaluated but of being over-valuated and deemed capable of mind-reading or of rendering curbstone solutions to multifarious problems.[39]"

And there are the challenges of dealing with the flood of idealization and devaluation they face in their everyday work with patients. Therapists then have to manage complicated and intense internal experiences of both self-doubt and grandiosity. Therefore, Yalom advises that therapists undertake repeated personal therapy and also create or join a therapist support group that allows for the sharing of the stresses of personal and professional life. Yalom says that he has always considered psychotherapy to be more of a calling than a profession. He advises people who are more interested in accumulating wealth than being of service to choose a different career.

He ends *The Gift of Therapy* with reflections on how being a therapist has been meaningful to him and to others in the profession: "Life as a therapist is a life of service in which we daily transcend our personal wishes and turn our gaze towards the needs and growth of the other . . . We take pleasure not only in the growth of our patient but also in the ripple effect—the salutary influence our patients have upon those whom they touch in life.[40]"

"Every day patients grace us with their secrets, often never before shared. Receiving such secrets is a privilege given to very few. The secrets provide a backstage view of the human condition without social frills, role-playing, bravado, or stage posturing. . . . Those who are cradlers of secrets are granted a clarifying lens through which to view the world—a view with less distortion, denial and illusion, a view of the way things really are. [We are] blessed by a clarity of vision into the true and tragic knowledge of the human condition.[41]

"We are intellectually challenged. We become explorers immersed in the grandest and most complex of pursuits—the development, functioning, and maintenance of the human mind. Hand-in-hand with patients, we savor the pleasure of great discoveries—the 'ah ha' experience when disparate ideational fragments suddenly slide smoothly together into coherence. At other times we are midwife to the birth of something new, liberating, and elevating. We watch our patients let go of old self-defeating patterns, detach from ancient grievances, develop zest for living, learn to love us and, through that act, turn lovingly to others. It is a joy to see others open the taps to their own founts of wisdom. Sometimes I feel like a guide escorting patients through the rooms of their own house. What a treat it is to watch them open doors to rooms never before entered, discover new wings of their house containing parts in exile—wise, beautiful, and creative pieces of identity . . .

"It has always struck me as an extraordinary privilege to belong to the venerable and honorable guild of healers. We therapists are part of a tradition reaching back not only to our immediate psychotherapy ancestors, beginning with Freud and Jung and all *their* ancestors, Nietzsche, Schopenhauer, Kierkegaard, but also to Jesus, the Buddha, Plato, Socrates, Galen, Hippocrates, and all the other great religious leaders, philosophers, and physicians who have, since the beginning of time, ministered to human despair.[42]"

# 6

# Yalom's Reflections on His Work

*Ruthellen:* I am impressed by how much philosophy you have read and integrated in your work as a therapist and a writer.

*Irv Yalom:* I spent 10 years reading philosophical works and writing *Existential Psychotherapy.* It was a good friend, Alex Comfort (a man known for *The Joy of Sex* but who wrote over fifty scholarly and literary books), who advised me it was time to stop reading and start writing. But I've continued to read philosophy ever since. *Existential Psychotherapy* was a sourcebook for all that I've written since then. All the books of stories and the novels were ways of expanding one or the other aspects of *Existential Psychotherapy.*

*Ruthellen:* But you don't think about Existential Psychotherapy as being a school of psychotherapy?

*Irv Yalom:* No. I never have. You cannot simply be trained as an existential psychotherapist. One has to be a well-trained therapist and then set about developing a sensitivity to existential issues. I've always resisted the idea of starting an institute or a training program. I have such a strong pull towards writing. I really love to write.

*Ruthellen:* With the widespread success of your case story books and then your first novel, did you then start writing more to the general public?

*Irv Yalom:* No, I always thought my audience was the young therapist, young residents in psychiatry and student psychologists and counselors.

*Ruthellen:* So you never thought about writing to the general public? They would be eavesdropping as you spoke to therapists.

*Irv Yalom:* Yes, they would be eavesdropping because they had been in therapy or were interested in the topic of therapy. I think the *Love's Executioner* book description proclaimed that this book was for people on both sides of the couch. And I also thought people in philosophy would be interested, especially in the Nietzsche book and the Schopenhauer.

That psychobiography of Schopenhauer was original—there's no other work like that.

*Ruthellen:* How come you chose Schopenhauer? With Nietzsche it's clearer to me, because you are so close to his philosophy.

*Irv Yalom:* Schopenhauer was always in the background. You have to remember that he was Nietzsche's teacher. (I mean intellectually—they never met.) But Nietzsche turned against him eventually and that break fascinated me for a long time. It was of great interest to me that they started from the same point, the same observations about the human condition, but one became life-celebrating and one life-negating. So what was that all about? I suspected it was driven by character, or personality, issues.

And also Freud was interested in Schopenhauer. He was the major German philosopher when Freud was educated. A great many of Freud's major ideas are sketched out in Schopenhauer's work. His work was very rich. He wrote voluminously about so many other topics such as politics, musicology, and esthetics but I concentrated solely on his writings about life and existence.

You have to recognize the human condition before you can figure out how to deal with it. Schopenhauer can inform us about the futility of desire and the inevitably of oblivion, but eventually it's the Nietzschean idea of embracing life that is the viable answer to this dilemma.

*Ruthellen:* In so many of your stories as well as the novels, there is a recurrence of the themes of sex obsession and love obsession. Can you tell me about how come this captured your interest?

*Irv Yalom:* I've always been struck with the idea of romantic love and losing oneself in the other in that way, which I've often characterized as "the lonely I dissolving into the we." And therefore you lose the sense of personal separateness and find comfort in the lack of loneliness. That's why I've always been intrigued with Otto Rank's formulation of going back and forth between the poles of life anxiety and death anxiety. And also Ernest Becker, who is very Rankian, and developed Rank's ideas in his wonderful book, *The Denial of Death*.

So I've always been interested in this idea of romantic love and also in religious submission, which is similar—both relate to the ultimate concern of isolation. And this issue of obsession was a predominant theme in Nietzsche.

I had a patient recently who was obsessed about a woman who had broken off with him but he couldn't get her out of his mind and he went and read the Nietzsche book and came back and said it did him more good than the two years of therapy we had done.

*Ruthellen:* So we strive to be autonomous but have difficulty dealing with our separateness?

*Irv Yalom:* Yes, and also underneath much compulsive activity is a lot of death anxiety. Often the death anxiety is overlooked because of other issues such as rage.

*Ruthellen:* So in the pain of existential isolation, the lonely I is connected to rage, which is connected to death anxiety. And the fear and the rage is about both aloneness and death. We are thrown into this finite existence alone. In your Nietzsche novel and in some of the stories, the aim is to help people give up the obsession.

*Irv Yalom:* Helping them find some more authentic way of relating to others.

*Ruthellen:*  Do you see love obsession and sex obsession as the same thing?

*Irv Yalom:*  I see them as first cousins. In *The Schopenhauer Cure*, Phillip's anxiety was assuaged by the sexual coupling, but the relief was evanescent. In romantic love, life can't be lived without this person and if you lose her, you're in continual grief—that's been the problem for many of my patients.

*Ruthellen:*  How do you distinguish between authentic meaningful connection and love obsession?

*Irv Yalom:*  The basic distinction lies in rationality, not thinking in irrational terms. A love obsession is highly irrational. It's ascribing things to the other that aren't there, not seeing the other as the other is, not being able to see the other person as a finite, separate person who doesn't have magical powers. A love obsession comes from the same stuff as religion, ascribing powers to the other.

*Ruthellen:*  Don't you think that when people love one another, they do some of that—a certain amount of idealizing, making the other person very special?

*Irv Yalom:*  I think that a true love relationship is caring for the being and becoming of the other person and having accurate empathy for the other person where you are trying to care for the other person in every way you can. But that may not be the focus of a love obsession. Like the first story in *Love's Executioner*— where one of the dyad did not even know the other was having a psychotic experience. People will fall in love with someone they hardly know. In true love, you see the other person accurately as a human being like yourself. You fall in love with someone by seeing who they are and what they are so they aren't forced to be someone they're not. For me, the kind of love relationship I want to espouse is one where one's eyes are wide open.

*Ruthellen:* So that would be a measure of the rationality of the relationship.

*Irv Yalom:* Yes.

*Ruthellen:* In your most recent book, *Staring at the Sun*, you return to the theme of death? I wonder why now?

*Irv Yalom:* I'm dealing more with this because of my age. I'm 76 now, an age when people die and I see my friends aging and dying. I see myself on

borrowed time. I spoke about much of this
in *Staring at the Sun*.

*Ruthellen:* What has it meant to write this book at this
age?

*Irv Yalom:* I've been so inured, so plunged into the topic.
Originally I was going to write a series of
connected fictional stories about dealing
with death anxiety. I had been reading a lot
of Plato and Epicurus and I thought I would
write a series of stories with some connection.
I was inspired by a Murukami book called
*After the Quake* in which all the stories were
connected by one thing: the Kobe earthquake.
I had six stories in mind and my plan was to
start each story with the identical nightmare
about death. In each story the dreamer wakes
up in a panic about dying, leaves the house
and searches for someone who can help him
with his death anxiety. The first story was set
in 348 BC and the dreamer goes out in search
of Epicurus. A second story would involve a
minor Pope of the middle ages, then in Freud's
time, then more contemporary stories. But I
spent so much time researching the first story
on Epicurus, reading about what the ancient
Greeks had for breakfast—what's a Greek café
like, what clothing was worn, then I started
reading novels about ancient Greece, a novel

about Archimedes, and about the priestesses at Delphi—until six months had elapsed and I realized that the background research would take years and I reluctantly gave up the idea, which I thought was a splendid concept. Perhaps one of the readers of this interview will write it some day.

So I went to the other project I had in mind, a revision of *Existential Psychotherapy.* I reread it carefully and underlined things I wanted to change and organized a course of students who would read it with me and help me to select the dated material, but, in the end, I was overwhelmed by the task, especially the scope of the library research looking up the empirical research on the ultimate concerns that has been accumulating in the twenty-five years since I first published this book. So I gave that up and wrote a book on what I had learned about an existential approach in the years that have passed since I wrote the text-book. Next my agent, noting that seventy-five per cent of the book addressed death anxiety, suggested that I might write a tighter book if I concentrated only on death anxiety. Finally the book underwent one more metamorphosis when my publisher suggested I direct it more to the general public. I agreed to do so but insisted upon a final chapter directed at

therapists. I believe the strongest chapter is
a personal chapter dealing with the development of my own awareness of death.

*Ruthellen:* Would you say that doing this book makes
you even less fearful about death than when
you started it?

*Irv Yalom:* I think so. But writing about death anxiety
wasn't an effort to heal myself about it. I've
never been that consumed with death anxiety. It was more of an issue a long time ago
when I started working with cancer patients. I
don't think I'm unusual in my degree of death
anxiety. Over the years, I feel like I've become
effective in dealing with patients with death
anxiety and am confident that I can offer help.

Irv shared with me a number of email letters he gets
daily from people all over the world. These are heartfelt
(often heart-rending) letters from people expressing
their appreciation of the ways in which his writings have
changed their lives.

"It is not enough to say that your words moved me or
affected me. When at the end [of *The Schopenhauer Cure*]
Pam placed her hands on Phillip and told him what he
needed to hear—the words on the page began to blur, all
I could do was lean my head back, swipe at the onslaught
of tears and wait for my faculties to return. It was the
catharsis I needed." Or from another: "I know I am alone

and finite, but I feel connected to the rest of humanity in reading your books because everyone else, I realize, is in the same boat—and thanks for that insight/comfort." And from a professor in Turkey: "I'm writing to you in appreciation of keeping me excellent company through the rough hours of the day: when you are alone, or even worse (better?) when you think you are alone . . . I usually start my lessons with a saying or a thought of yours in order to boost my class—and me—to open a new window and see things a little bit different."

Other letters are from people longing to find some salve for their emotional pain, some of what he has provided his own patients. He answers each of these letters personally, acknowledging their meaning for him or, when he can, offering counsel.

*Ruthellen:* What have these letters meant to you?

*Irv Yalom:* I feel I have another, a second therapy practice. I know I mean a lot to some of my readers. I'm aware that they imbue me with a lot more wisdom than I have and they long to connect with me. I try to answer every letter, even if it's just to say thank you for your note. This correspondence makes me unusually aware of my readership. I took an early retirement from the Department of Psychiatry fifteen years ago. One of my main reasons was that psychiatry had become so re-medicalized that my students had little interest in psycho-

therapy and instead were far more interested
in biochemistry and pharmacological research
and practice. I didn't really have students who
were interested in what I had to teach. So I
now feel that my teaching is done through
my writing. I don't miss classroom teaching
because I feel that I now have this whole
other way of teaching. I consider my writing
teaching and getting this correspondence
keeps me aware of that all the time.

*Ruthellen:* What message do you try to convey in
response?

*Irv Yalom:* As I said, some simply express appreciation
for the writing or tell me it was meaningful to
them and I simply state that I feel good that
my writing had a positive impact. Sometimes
I say that writers send their books out like
ships at sea and that I'm delighted that a book
arrived at the right port.

There are other readers who ask for help for
some personal issue and, if appropriate, I urge
them to seek therapy. Some write a second
time thanking me for being instrumental in
their obtaining help. Some readers comment
that their current therapy isn't helping and
ask for email therapy. I don't do therapy by
email and urge them to be direct with their

therapist and to express these sentiments openly. I even suggest that concealing these feelings may be instrumental in their therapy not being useful. Their job in therapy is to share all their feelings and wishes with their therapists. Able therapists will welcome this forthrightness. My main message though is to let them know that I've read their letter.

*Ruthellen:* It makes me so sad to hear that you had students who didn't want to learn what you had to teach. What does this say about the future of psychotherapy?

*Irv Yalom:* I do feel there is a pendulum swinging, even in psychiatry. I do hear about more programs starting to introduce therapy again. Many contemporary therapists are trained in manualized mechanical modes—all of which eschew the authentic encounter. After some years of practice, however, a great many of these therapists come to appreciate the superficiality of their approach and yearn for something deeper, something more far-reaching and lasting. At this time therapists enter postgraduate therapy training programs or supervision. Or they learn by entering their own therapy. And I can assure you they never *never* seek a therapist who practices mechanical, behavioral or manualized therapy. They go in search of a genuine encounter that will recognize the challenge inherent in facing the human condition.

# Afterword

In 2005, Irv and I went to visit Jerome Frank, Irv's mentor and friend, who lived in a nursing home nearby my own home in Baltimore. We had been visiting him, separately and together, over many years, as he steadily declined with age. Even as his physical and mental impairments progressed, Jerry was always professorially dressed in suit and tie. "Tell me what you're working on," Jerry would usually ask Irv when we arrived, and they would embark on lively conversation about Irv's work and whatever Jerry was reading at the time. (My role was usually to sit and smile and enjoy the warmth of their connection. I knew Jerry far less well and for less long, of course.) On this particular occasion, Jerry was not wearing his suit and, after a few moments, it became clear that his mental decline was far worse. In fact, we soon realized that he didn't know who we were. I was very embarrassed and unsure what to do, and I left the conversational challenge to Irv. He tried a few topics to engage Jerry and found that Jerry could still remember some people from the distant past and they talked some about them. But then, Irv's genius asserted itself in the flow of this difficult interaction and he asked, kindly and compassionately, "What is like for you, Jerry, to be sitting here talking to people when you aren't sure who we are?" Always the here and now! And Jerry understood and responded to the care in the question. "I'm glad of the company," he said, "and you know, it's not so bad. Each day I wake up and see outside my window the trees and the flowers and I'm happy to see them. It's not so bad." Once again, Irv had penetrated to the existential core of Jerry's experience, and he did so by daring to speak the simple reality of our being together. Perhaps the message of his whole corpus of work is just this. It's all we have.

# Works by Irvin D. Yalom

BOOKS

Yalom, I.D., *The Theory and Practice of Group Psychotherapy*. New York: Basic Books, 1970.

Lieberman, M.A., Yalom, I.D., Miles, M.B., *Encounter Groups: First Facts*. New York: Basic Books, 1973.

Yalom, I.D., Elkins, Ginny, *Everyday Gets a Little Closer*. New York: Basic Books, 1974.

Yalom, I.D., *The Theory and Practice of Group Psychotherapy*. New York: Second edition, Basic Books, 1975.

Yalom, I.D., *Existential Psychotherapy*. New York: Basic Books, 1980.

Yalom, I.D., *Inpatient Group Psychotherapy*. New York: Basic Books, 1983.

Yalom, I.D., *The Theory and Practice of Group Psychotherapy*, Third Edition. New York: Basic Books, 1985.

Yalom, I.D., *Love's Executioner and Other Tales of Psychotherapy*. New York: Basic Books, 1989. Paperback Harper Collins, 1990.

Yalom, I.D., Vinogradov, S., *Concise Guide to Group Psychotherapy*. American Psychiatric Press, Inc. Washington, D.C., 1989.

Yalom, I.D., *When Nietzsche Wept*. New York: Basic Books/Harper, 1991. Paperback: HarperCollins, 1992 (Commonwealth Club of California Gold Medal for best fiction of 1993.)

Yalom, I.D., *The Theory and Practice of Group Psychotherapy*, Fourth Edition, 1995. New York: Basic Books.

Yalom, I.D., *Lying on the Couch*, Basic Books, 1996, New York.

Yalom, I.D., *The Yalom Reader*, Basic Books, 1998, New York.

Yalom, I.D., *Momma and the Meaning of Life*, Basic Books, 1999, New York.

Yalom, I.D., *The Gift of Therapy*, HarperCollins Publishers, 2002, New York.

Yalom, I.D., *The Schopenhauer Cure*, HarperCollins Publishers, 2005, New York.

Yalom, I.D., *The Theory and Practice of Group Psychotherapy*, Fifth Edition, Basic Books, May, 2005, New York.

Yalom, I.D., *Staring at the Sun: Overcoming the Terror of Death*. Jossey-Bass, 2008, San Francisco.

VIDEO TAPES

*Understanding Group Therapy.* Three Volume, Five Tape Videotape
Series (Volume One—outpatient groups; Volume Two—inpa-
tient groups; Volume Three—interview). Brooks Cole Publishing
Pacific Grove, Ca. Distributed by Victor Yalom through
Psychotherapy.net .
*Irvin Yalom: Live Case Consultation.* Distributed by Victor Yalom
through Psychotherapy.net .
*The Gift of Therapy, a Conversation with Irvin Yalom, M.D.*
Distributed by Victor Yalom through Psychotherapy.net .

ARTICLES, CHAPTERS

1.   Yalom, I., "Lysergic acid diethylamide," *Maryland State Medical Journal,* 8:14–17, 1959.
2.   Yalom, I., "Aggression and forbiddenness in voyeurism," *Archives of General Psychiatry,* 3:305–319, 1960.
3.   Yalom, I., "Organic brain diseases of senility," *Maryland State Medical Journal,* December, 1960.
4.   Yalom, I., "Group therapy of Incarcerated Sexual Deviants," *Journal of Nerve and Mental Disorders,* 132:158–170, 1961.
5.   Jackson, D. and Yalom, I., "Family homeostasis and patient changes," *Current Psychiatric Therapies,* IV:155–165, 1964.
6.   Yalom, I., "Planter warts: a case study," *Journal of Nerve and Mental Disorders,* 1964.
7.   Yalom, I., "Observation on mourning," *The New Physician,* 13:80–81, 1964.
8.   Yalom, I. and Moos, R., "The use of small interactional groups in the teaching of psychiatry," *International Journal of Group Psychotherapy,* 15:242–250, 1965.
9.   Jackson, D. and Yalom, I., "Conjoint family therapy as an aid to intensive psychotherapy," in Burton, A. (Ed.) *Modern Psychotherapeutic Practice,* Palo Alto, CA: Science and Behavior Books, Inc., pp. 81–99, 1965.
10.  Yalom, I., "Problems of neophyte group therapists," *International Journal of Social Psychiatry,* 7:52–59, 1966.
11.  Yalom, I., "A study of group therapy dropouts," *Archives of General Psychiatry,* 14:393–414, 1966.
12.  Yalom, I. and Handlon, J., "The use of multiple therapists in the teaching of psychiatric residents," *Journal of Nerve and Mental Disorders,* 141:684–692, 1966.
13.  Moos, R. and Yalom, I., "Medical students attitudes toward psychiatry and psychiatrists," *Mental Hygiene,* 50:246–256, 1966.
14.  Yalom, I. and Rand, K., "Compatibility and cohesiveness in therapy groups," *Archives of General Psychiatry,* 15:267–275, 1966.
15.  Jackson, D. and Yalom, I., "Family research on the problem of ulcerative colitis," *Archives of General Psychiatry,* 15:410–418, 1966.

16. Yalom, I., "Some aspects of symptom removal," *Short Circuit*, 1, 1966.
17. Yalom, I., Houts, P., Zimerberg, S., Rand, K., "Prediction in improvement in group therapy: an exploratory study," *Archives of General Psychiatry*, 17:159–169, 1967.
18. Yalom, I., Houts, P., Newell, G., Rand, K., "Preparation of patients for group therapy: a controlled study," *Archives of General Psychiatry*, 17:416–427, 1967.
19. Hamburg, D., Moos, R., Yalom, I., "Studies of premenstrual and postpartum distress," in Michael, R. (Ed.) *Endocrinology and Human Behavior*, New York: Oxford University Press, pp. 94–116, 1968.
20. Yalom, I., Lunde, D., Moos, R., Hamburg, D., "Postpartum blues syndrome: a description and related variables," *Archives of General Psychiatry*, 18:16–27, 1968.
21. Yalom, I. and Terrazas, F., "Group therapy for psychotic elderly patients," *American Journal of Nursing*, August 1968, 1960–1964.
22. Ebersole, G., Leiderman, P., Yalom, I., "Training the non-professional group therapist: a controlled study," *Journal of Nervous Mental Disorders*, 149:294–302, 1969.
23. Moos, R., Kopell, B., Melges, F., Yalom, I., Lunde, D., Clayton, R., Hamburg, D., "Fluctuations in symptoms and moods during the menstrual cycle," *Journal of Psychosomatic Research*, 13:37–44, 1969.
24. Sklar, A., Yalom, I., Zimerberg, S., Newell, G., "Time-extended group therapy: a controlled study," *Comparative Group Studies*, November 1970, 373–386.
25. Lieberman, M., Yalom, I., Miles, M., "The group experience project: a comparison of ten encounter technologies," in L. Blank, M. Gottsegen, G. Gottsegen (Eds.) *Encounter*, New York: The MacMillan Company, 1971.
26. Yalom, I. and Yalom, M., Hemingway: "A Psychiatric View," *Archives of General Psychiatry*, 24:485–494, 1971.
27. Yalom, I., "A study of encounter group casualties," *Archives of General Psychiatry*, 25:16–30, 1971.
28. Leiberman, M., Yalom, I., Miles, M., "Impact on participants," *New Perspectives on Encounter Groups*, Solomon and Berzon, Jossey-Bass, Inc., pp. 119–170, 1972.
29. Yalom, I., Moffat, S., "Instant intimacy," *Encyclopædia Britannica*, pp. 408–423, *Britannica Yearbook of Science and the Future*, 1972, Encyclopædia Britannica, Inc.
30. Lieberman, M., Yalom, I., Miles, M., "The impact of encounter groups on participants: some preliminary findings," *The Journal of Applied Behavioral Sciences*, 8:1, 1972.
31. Costell, Ronald, M., Yalom, I., "The institutional treatment of sex offenders," in Resnik and Wolfgang (Eds.) *Treatment of the Sexual Offender*, New York: Little, Brown and Co., 1972.
32. Yalom, I., "The future of group therapy," in Hamburg and Brodie (Eds.) *The American Handbook of Psychiatry*, Vol 6, New York: Basic Books, 1973.

33. Yalom, I., Green, R., Fisk, N., "Intrauterine female hormone exposure and psychosexual development in human males," *Archives of General Psychiatry*, Vol 28, 1973.

34. Yalom, I., "Freud, group psychology and group psychotherapy," *International Journal of Group Psychotherapy*, Vol XXIV, No. 1, January 1974.

35. Yalom, I., "Group therapy and alcoholism," *Annals of the New York Academy of Sciences*, 233:85–103, 1974.

36. Yalom, I., Brown, S., Bloch, S., "The written summary as a group psychotherapy technique," *Archives of General Psychiatry*, 32:605–613, 1975.

37. Yalom, I., "Using the here-and-now in group therapy," *Proceedings of the Third Annual Conference of the Group Therapy Department*, Washington Square Institute for Psychotherapy and Mental Health, May 1976.

38. Bloch, S., Bond, G., Qualls, B., Yalom, I., Zimmerman, E., "Patients expectations of therapeutic improvement and their outcomes," *American Journal of Psychiatry*, 133:12, December 1976, pp. 1457–1460.

39. Yalom, I., Bond, G., Bloch, S., Zimmerman, E., Friedmand, L., "The impact of a weekend group experience on individual therapy," *Archives of General Psychiatry*, Vol 34, April 1977, pp. 399–415.

40. Yalom, I., "Existential factors in group psychotherapy," in O. L. McCabe (Ed.) *Changing Human Behavior: Current Therapies and Future Directions*, Grune & Stratton, September 1977.

41. Bloch, S., Bond, G., Qualls, B., Yalom, I., Zimmerman, E., "The evaluation of outcome in psychotherapy by independent judges: a new approach," *British Journal of Psychiatry*, 131:410–414, 1977.

42. Yalom, I., Greaves, C., "Group therapy with the terminally ill," *American Journal of Psychiatry*, 134:4, April 1977, pp. 396–400.

43. Brown, S., Yalom, I., "Interactional group therapy with alcoholics," *Journal of Studies on Alcohol*, 38:3, March 1977, pp. 426–456.

44. Spiegel, D., Yalom, I., "A support group for dying patients," *International Journal of Group Psychotherapy*, 28:2, April 1978.

45. Yalom, I., Bloch, S., Bond, G., Zimmerman, E., Qualls, B., "Alcoholics in interactional group therapy: an outcome study," *Archives of General Psychiatry*, 35:419–425, April 1978.

46. Bond, G., Bloch, S., Yalom, I., Zimmerman, E., Qualls, B., "The evaluation of a 'Target problem' approach to outcome measurement," *Psychotherapy, Theory, Research and Practice*, 16:1, Spring 1979.

47. Spiegel, D., Bloom, J., Yalom, I., "Group support for metastatic cancer patients: a randomized prospective outcome study," *Archives of General Psychiatry*, 38:527–534, May 1981.

48. Finkelstein, P., Wenegrat, B., Yalom, I., "Large group awareness training," in *Annual Review of Psychology*, 33:515–539, 1982.

49. May, R., Yalom, I., "Existential psychotherapy," in R. Corsini (Ed.)," *Current Psychotherapies*, Third edition, 1985.

50. Leszcz, M., Yalom, I., Norden, M., "The value of inpatient group psychotherapy and therapeutic process: patients perceptions," *International Journal of Group Psychotherapy*, Vol 35, July 1985.

51. Yalom, I., "Interpersonal learning," in *American Psychiatric Association Annual Review: Vol V* American Psychiatric Press, Inc., 1986.

52. Yalom, I.D., Vinogradov, S., "Bereavement groups: techniques and themes," *International Journal of Group Psychotherapy*, 38:4, October 1988.

53. Yalom, I., Vinogradov, S., "Self-disclosure in group therapy," *Self-disclosure in the Therapeutic Relationship* ed. by G. Stricker and M. Fisher, Plenum Press, N.Y. 1990.

54. Yalom, I.D., Yalom, V., "Brief Interactional group psychotherapy," *Annals of Psychiatry*, 1990

55. Yalom, I.D., Matano, R., "Chemical dependency and interactional group therapy: a synthesis," *International Journal of Group Psychotherapy*, July 1991 p269–295

56. Yalom, I.D., Lieberman, M., "Bereavement and heightened existential awareness," *Psychiatry* 1992.

57. Lieberman, M., Yalom, I.D., "Brief psychotherapy for the spousally bereaved: A Controlled Study," *International Journal of Group Psychotherapy*, vol 42, Jan 1992.

58. Luby, J., Yalom, I.D., "Group therapy of depressive disorders," E.S. Paykel (Ed.) *Handbook of Affective Disorders:2E*, Guilford Press, Churchill-Livingstone, June, 1992.

59. Yalom, I., Vinogradov, S., "Group therapy," in *Textbook of Psychiatry*, American Psychiatric Press, (Hales, Yudofsky, Talbot (eds) Wash D.C. 2nd ed. 1994.

60. Rogers, Carl, *A Way of Being*, Houghton Mifflin (1995), Introduction by Irvin D. Yalom.

61. Yalom, I., Vinogradov, S., "Group therapy," in *Synopsis of Psychiatry*, American Psychiatric Press, Wash. D.C. 1996 page 1063–1097.

62. Rabinowitz, Ilana, *Inside Therapy*, St. Martins Press (1998), Introduction by Irvin D. Yalom.

63. Breuer, Josef and Freud, Sigmund, *Studies in Hysteria*, Basic Books (2000), Introduction by Irvin D. Yalom.

# Endnotes

## Guide to Works in Endnotes:

EP = *Existential Psychotherapy*
SC = *The Schopenhauer Cure*
YR = *The Yalom Reader*
GT = *The Gift of Therapy*
STS = *Staring at the Sun*

1   Interview material in this chapter and in chapter 6 is taken from interviews conducted in 2007. Yalom has read and edited all the interview material.
2   In his most recent (5th) edition, the task of assimilating the current professional literature was taken over by a colleague, a former student, Molyn Leszcz M.D.
3   EP, p. 291
4   EP, p. 137
5   Allen Wheelis was an existential psychoanalyst who wrote many books. The following story is adapted from his book *The Listener* (Norton, 1999).
6   Pfister Lecture, 2002, available at www.yalom.com
7   STS, p. 5
8   EP, p. 145
9   EP, pp. 117–8
10  It is interesting that his early mentor, Jerome Frank, had been the first recipient of the Oscar Pfister prize.
11  Pfister Lecture, 2002.
12  STS, p. 194
13  STS, p. 197
14  STS, p. 7
15  STS, p. 83
16  STS, p. 201
17  Pfister Lecture, 2002.
18  STS, p. 201
19  LE Foreword
20  Adapted from *When Nietzsche Wept*
21  STS, p. 206.
22  Nietzsche, *The Gay Science*, p. 14, cited in YR, p. 379.

23  SC, p. 1
24  SC, p. 99
25  SC, p. 100
26  SC, pp. 288–9
27  SC, p. 331
28  YR, p. 414
29  YR, p. 420
30  YR, p. 421
31  GT, p. 17–18
32  GT, p. 26
33  GT, p. 30
34  GT, p. 233
35  GT, pp. 232–3
36  GT, pp. 222–3
37  GT, p. 223
38  GT, p. 251
39  GT, p. 252
40  GT, p. 256
41  GT, p. 257
42  GT, pp. 258–9